CREATIVE
BIBLE LESSONS
IN
1 & 2 TIMOTHY
AND TITUS

12 Sessions
to Deepen Your
Faith in a World of
Oppression, Danger,
and Difficulty

Perfect for
Sunday school,
youth meetings,
small groups,
and more!

LEN EVANS

ZONDERVAN™

WWW.ZONDERVAN.COM

Youth Specialties
www.youthspecialties.com

Creative Bible Lessons in 1 & 2 Timothy and Titus
Copyright © 2004 by Youth Specialties

Youth Specialties Books, 300 South Pierce Street, El Cajon, CA 92020, are published by Zondervan, 5300 Patterson Avenue SE, Grand Rapids, MI 49530

Library of Congress Cataloging-in-Publication Data

Case, Steve L., 1964-
 Everything counts : a years worth of devotions on radical living / by
Steven L. Case.
    p. cm.
Incorporates excerpts from the writings of Oswald Chambers.
Summary: Bible verses and text for each day of the year provide guidance
along a faith journey which has, as its goal, absolute and entire
dovotion of oneself to God.
 ISBN 0-310-25408-6
 1. Christian teenagers--Religious life--Juvenile literature. 2.
Christian life--Biblical teaching--Juvenile literature. 3. Devotional
calendars--Juvenile literature. [1. Christian life. 2. Devotional
calendars.] I. Chambers, Oswald, 1874-1917. II. Title.
 BV4531.3.C37 2003
 248.8'3--dc21

2003005831

Editing by Laura Gross
Cover design by Brian Smith
Interior design by Holly Sharp
Printed in the United States of America

04 05 06 07 08 09 / DC / 10 9 8 7 6 5 4 3 2 1

ACKNOWLEDGMENTS

Without my family, friends, and prayer team, this book would not exist. I have had nothing but support and encouragement regarding this project from my parents, my brother Art, my in-laws, and my immediate family. Special thanks to Taylor and Sarabeth for all the laughter and love they have given me. Daddy can now play more on his days off!

This book is dedicated to my wife, Tonja, who epitomizes being the "better half" in practically every area. Thank you for believing in me and for sharing your love and life with me for all these years. I am confident that God brought us together, and I can't wait to see where he will take us.

CONTENTS

introduction

HOW TO USE THIS BOOK

To get the most out of this book you'll need to spend some time with it as you prepare your lesson. Most of us have experienced those times when we are looking at a curriculum book on the way to the meeting (only reading it while we're waiting at red lights, of course) and praying, God, please help this lesson work. But if you do that consistently and the church pays you for your labors, eventually you might find yourself praying, God, please *find* me work!

If you spend an hour reading the lesson, choosing the options that fit your group, and inserting your own dash of creativity by adapting or adding something to it, then you'll be fully prepared. Hopefully you can spend at least 30 minutes doing those things and still get your copies made before class starts.

Movie Start Times
We've used the DVD version of these films to determine the movie clip start and stop times, which are all timed from the start of the actual movie—when the distribution company logo appears on the screen (20th Century Fox, and the like).

Lesson Breakdown
Each lesson contains the following parts—

> *The Big Idea:* A brief overview of the lesson's theme.

> *Background Check:* Helpful information about the setting for the Scripture passage(s). You may choose to incorporate this information into your lesson, or perhaps you'll just glean some interesting tidbits that will add a little flavor. Other times it'll just be FYI, and you won't choose to use it with your students at all.

> *Opening Options:* Typically you will be given two options for activities or ideas that will serve as a lesson warm-up to introduce the theme and help students interact with the story.

> *Read It in God's Word:* The meat of the lesson. The classic three-step approach to understanding a biblical text (as taught by Howard "The Prof" Hendricks of Dallas Theological Seminary) is Observation, Interpretation, and Application.

> > • Observation is merely discovering what the text says. So please read the Scripture text on your own so you know what it is saying.
> > • Interpretation is when you try to understand the context of the passage. Contexts include, but are not limited to, who was the author, what is the genre of literature, to whom was it written, when was it written, where was it written, the language in which it was written, the time in God's progressive revelation in which it was written, and more. This section offers interpretation in some areas and helps you wrestle with the interpretation in other areas.

Live It in Your World: Some ideas for the Application step.

Put It in Your Heart: The take-away verse for each lesson, which is either taken directly from the lesson or carries the theme of the lesson. Encourage your students to memorize it.

Small Group Questions: Use these any way you want to. They don't have to be used in small groups, but they can be. You could also use them during your large group time to create class interaction and discussion, or just use them rhetorically. Feel free to add your own questions based upon your understanding of the text and the application of the truths from God's Word.

Closing Prayer: Finish your study with a word of prayer. Allow enough time at the end of the meeting so your students will have an opportunity to pray not only for each other's specific prayer requests, but also for whatever they may need from the Lord that will help them apply what they've just learned out in the "real world."

I hope this resource is useful for you and your ministry. Thank you for the privilege of helping you as you continue to serve the God of the universe in the wondrous service called youth ministry.

Keep Serving the Savior,
Len Evans

paul's pastoral protégés

TALES OF TIMOTHY AND TITUS: FIRST-CENTURY TRUTHS FOR THE 21ST CENTURY

session 1

During this session students will—

- Discover how the lives of Paul, Timothy, and Titus intertwine and affect each other.
- Evaluate their own spiritual heritage and plan their spiritual legacy.

■ THE BIG IDEA

Both Timothy and Titus were pastors. They were very different from each other, yet God used both of them. God can also use you regardless of your background, gender, financial status, age, or anything else. The truths Paul shared in his letters to these two men will help everyone who reads them.

DID YOU KNOW?

WHAT'S A PASTORAL EPISTLE?

For around 200 years, "Pastoral Epistle" has been used to describe the grouping of 1 Timothy, 2 Timothy, and Titus. These three books of the Bible go together like the flavors in Neapolitan ice cream.

■ BACKGROUND CHECK

It is generally agreed that these books were written in this order—1 Timothy, Titus, and then 2 Timothy. The most likely scenario is that Paul was released from prison in Rome (as we last see him in Acts 28). After a few years of freedom, he was recaptured and finally killed in Rome. It's during these last three or four years of his life and ministry that Paul wrote the Pastoral Epistles. If 1 Timothy and Titus were written during the last leg of his race, 2 Timothy was written as he approached the finish line. It is often referred to as his "last will and testament."

Because they are so unlike the other Bible books Paul wrote—the vocabulary is very distinct, plus they were written to a person and not directly to a church (although they were to be used by the Church)—some scholars argue that he must not have written these three books. However, these contrasts simply indicate that these books were written for different purposes. We write a letter to a friend differently than we do a letter to our senator or a letter to the editor of the local paper. So it is with the Pastoral Epistles—they were written for the benefit of the church where Timothy and Titus had been assigned to work, but they were also within God's plan for the entire body of believers that would come and be part of the Church.

OPENING
Option 1: Great Partners

You'll need—
• Copies of **Great Partners Matching Game** (page 13), one for each pair of students
• Pen or pencil for each pair
• Candy bar prize for the winners

Ask students to pair off and then hand out copies of **Great Partners Matching Game** (page 13) and a pen or pencil to each twosome. Students should work together to complete the repro page; give them just two or three minutes to do so. Then go over the following answers with the group and award a candy bar prize to the team with the most correct answers: 1-R; 2-Q; 3-K; 4-N; 5-L; 6-T; 7-P; 8-J; 9-S; 10-B; 11-O; 12-A; 13-C; 14-F; 15-U; 16-G; 17-D; 18-M; 19-H; 20-I; 21-E.

Transition with something like this—

This was a fairly easy activity to do because all the partners on the list are not only well-known in their own right, but they are also known for being together. When you think of Paul, you should also think of his various ministry partners: Silas, Barnabas, Timothy, and Titus. Timothy and Titus stand out among even his closest associates because Paul wrote individual letters to each of them, which are included in our Bible. The books of 1 Timothy, 2 Timothy, and Titus are a trilogy and are referred to as the Pastoral Epistles.

Option 2: What Do You Look for in FRIENDS?

You'll need—
• Copies of **What Do You Look for in FRIENDS?** (page 14), one for each student
• Pen or pencil for each student

This activity will help your students think about the characteristics they look for—or maybe should look for—in their friends, as well as the kind of friend they should be to others. Pass out the **What Do You Look for in FRIENDS?** (page 14) and ask students to read the instructions before giving them five to 10 minutes to write down their answers. (Encourage them to write two answers for each letter if they have the time.)

Afterward you can transition with something like this—

When you think of Paul, you should also think of his various ministry partners: Silas, Barnabas, Timothy, and Titus. Timothy and Titus stand out among even his closest associates because Paul wrote individual letters to each of them, which are included in our Bible. The books of 1 Timothy, 2 Timothy, and Titus are a trilogy and are referred to as the Pastoral Epistles.

READ IT IN GOD'S WORD
In order for students to fully appreciate the relationships these men shared with each other, use the "Background Check" section, in addition to the following information, to explain some of the behind-the-scenes facts that intertwine and affect the lives of Paul, Timothy, and Titus.

Jesus and Paul

• Jesus sent out 72 of his followers in groups of two to minister to people. Paul continued this tradition by having many people help him in ministry and life: Barnabas, Silas, Luke, Mark, Apollos, Epaphroditus, and Aquila. The women included Priscilla, Lydia, Euodia, and Syntyche—and a lot of other women and men with names that are hard to pronounce.

• Jesus had his disciples, but of these 12 men, he had an inner circle of John, Peter, and James. And among these three, John had the closest relationship with Jesus—he calls himself "the disciple Jesus loved." Paul's inner circle would include Barnabas, Silas, Timothy, and Titus. But of them all, Timothy had the closest relationship with Paul.

Timothy and Titus

• We know very little about Titus. He was a Gentile believer who ministered and traveled with Paul (Galatians 2:1-3). He served in the troubled church in Corinth (2 Corinthians 8:16-24). Titus is last mentioned as being in Dalmatia (2 Timothy 4:10), or modern-day Yugoslavia, and tradition says he eventually returned to Crete and served there until his death.

• We don't know for certain, but it's reasonable to think of Timothy as being between the ages of 15 and 19 when he joined Paul in Acts 16. Therefore, he could have been around 30 or 34 years old when he was doing ministry in Ephesus.

ACTIVITY
INTERNSHIP IMAGINATION: BECOMING PROFESSIONAL IN YOUR PROFESSION

You'll need—
• Copies of **Internship Imagination** (page 15) for each student
• Pen or pencil for each student

Hand out the **Internship Imagination** page (page 15) and something to write with while you read the following instructions—

What do you want to be when you grow up? You've been asked that question throughout your life. Now imagine you get to choose someone—who is now either living or dead—to instruct you as to how to do the professions that are listed on this sheet. Who would you choose to be your instructor in each profession? Write down your answers.

When the activity is completed, ask students to break into smaller groups and explain to each other why they chose the person they did for their dream internship. Or ask a few students to share their responses with the entire group. Then ask, **What are the benefits and responsibilities of being mentored by someone great?**

• The key is to follow someone worth following. Timothy and Titus partnered with Paul in his ministry, and they learned from him how to be a Christian and how to be a minister or a pastor. It was very similar to what we would call an internship today. Now Timothy is going to mentor others by going to Corinth to represent Paul and his ministry.

• Ask a student to read this passage for the group—
"I hope in the Lord Jesus to send Timothy to you soon, that I also may be cheered when I receive news about you. I have no one else like him, who takes a genuine interest in your welfare. For everyone looks out for his own interests, not those of Jesus Christ. But you know that Timothy has proved himself, because as a son with his father he has served with me in the work of the gospel" (Philippians 2:19-22).
• "I have no one else like him"—Timothy is distinct. He stood out among the other followers of Christ. "The brothers…spoke well of him" (Acts 16:2). Would the adults in your church speak well of you? Would the adults in your church speak well of your youth ministry? Why or why not?
• "Who takes a genuine interest in your welfare"—Timothy cares for others. How well do you care for others?
• "But you know that Timothy has proved himself"—Timothy had a proven track record. Not just with Paul but

with other believers as well. How can you become more reliable?

• "Because as a son with his father"—Timothy is like a son to Paul. Paul never had children, but he refers to Timothy and Titus as sons. Do you have a spiritual father or mother who cares for you?

• "He has served with me in the work of the gospel"—Timothy is a servant of the gospel. All believers should serve in the work of the gospel in whatever way God has designed them.

• Ask a student to read this passage for the group—
"Fourteen years later I went up again to Jerusalem, this time with Barnabas. I took Titus along also. I went in response to a revelation and set before them the gospel that I preach among the Gentiles. But I did this privately to those who seemed to be leaders, for fear that I was running or had run my race in vain. Yet not even Titus, who was with me, was compelled to be circumcised, even though he was a Greek" (Galatians 2:1-3).

• Titus was a living illustration of grace! Acts 15:1-19 tells the full story (even though Titus is not mentioned). Timothy came from a mixed heritage, but Titus was not Jewish in any way. Believers of that day tried to combine their traditions of Judaism with their faith in Christ and his grace. It couldn't be done. They wanted non-Jews to be circumcised to prove they were believers. Titus was not circumcised because grace had arrived, and when grace is present, you don't add anything to the recipe of salvation.

ACTIVITY
LIFE TIME LINE CHART

You'll need—
• Two-sided copies of **Timothy's Time Line** and **Four Things That Change You** (pages 16-17) for each student
• Pen or pencil for each student
• Blank half sheets of paper for each student

Hand out copies of **Timothy's Time Line** (page 16) to your students and ask them to take a few minutes to read it individually. As they're looking it over, you may want to highlight a few of the items on the time line. Now ask them to turn their pages over to the side called **Four Things That Changed You** (page 17). Say something like—

> *You will pretty much be the same person you are today two, five, 10, even 20 years from now—except for the following four things:*
>   *1. Places you go*
>   *2. People you know*
>   *3. Experiences that cause you to grow*
>   *4. Books that cause you to grow*

Give students five minutes to write their answers for each item.

Now...using the half pieces of paper you provide for them, your students should use their responses to create a time line for their own lives. The hope is that by working on this project, the students will be able to take a step back and not only see how far God has brought them, but also realize that he isn't done with them yet.

LIVE IT IN YOUR WORLD

Say something like—

> *Timothy had a rich spiritual history through his mother and grandmother; but being from a Gentile family, Titus did not have this privilege. God used both men, but one benefited from a godly legacy. What kind of legacy will you leave?*

Read **Jonathan Edward's Legacy** (page 18) aloud to your group. Now say—

We talked earlier about WHAT you want to be when you grow up. Now we want to figure out WHO you want to be when you grow up. Use the back of the half sheets of paper—or the internship repro pages we did earlier—and respond to these instructions.

1. Name four places you think would change you if you visited them.
2. List four people with the potential to have a great impact on your life over the next couple of years.
3. Briefly describe four "mountaintop" experiences that you'd like to have.
4. List four ways that "valley" experiences might occur in your future.
5. List four books that you've heard good things about and want to read.

(Note: You could also project these questions onto a screen or blank wall using PowerPoint or an overhead for all the kids to see.)

PUT IT IN YOUR HEART
The brothers…spoke well of [Timothy] (Acts 16:2).

SMALL GROUP QUESTIONS
1. Would your lifestyle remind people of a life in Christ Jesus?
2. Who is your best friend and why?
3. Do you have different best friends depending on where you are—school, work, church, or after-school activities?
4. Do you have an older person who is your primary mentor or encourager for your faith?
5. Who helps you grow in your faith?
6. How do they help you in your faith?
7. Who would you choose to be your mentor about how to be successful? Explain.
8. Who would you choose to be your mentor about how to be spiritual? Explain.
9. Do you need a *spiritual mentor*?
10. Do you feel more like Timothy (strong Christian family) or Titus (mixed spiritual heritage)?
11. Do you have a spiritual parent in your life? (A spiritual parent is someone who looks after you spiritually the same way your parents look after you otherwise.)
12. What are the benefits of being someone's apprentice?
13. Good training doesn't equal perfection, but it does allow you to be more prepared. What are you doing in your life now to prepare for the future?

CLOSING PRAYER

GREAT PARTNERS MATCHING GAME

On the line to the left of each numbered person below, write down the letter that appears next to the name of each person's buddy, pal, sidekick, or partner in crime from the right-hand column.

1. Moe	A. Randy and Paula
2. Batman	B. Huck
3. Snoopy	C. Ernie
4. Chris Farley	D. Kevin Eubanks
5. J.Lo	E. Costello
6. Calvin	F. Grace
7. Spider-Man	G. Jill
8. Mickey	H. Tonto
9. Popeye	I. Hardy
10. Tom	J. Minnie
11. Bonnie	K. Charlie Brown
12. Simon	L. Too many to count
13. Bert	M. Timmy
14. Will	N. David Spade
15. Ken	O. Clyde
16. Jack	P. Mary Jane
17. Jay Leno	Q. Robin
18. Lassie	R. Larry and Curly
19. The Lone Ranger	S. Olive
20. Laurel	T. Hobbes
21. Abbott	U. Barbie

WHAT DO YOU LOOK FOR IN FRIENDS?

Create a personalized acronym for the word FRIENDS. Use words that begin with each capitalized letter to create a list of seven different qualities that you believe are important for any friend to have—including yourself. Use two words for each letter if you have time.

F _____

R _____

I _____

E _____

N _____

D _____

S _____

INTERNSHIP IMAGINATION

Becoming Professional in Your Profession

What do you want to be when you grow up? You've been asked that question throughout your life; now imagine you get to choose someone who is living or dead to instruct you as to how to work in the following professions. Who would you choose to be your instructors? Put a star next to the profession that you would consider to be your *dream internship*.

Profession	Professional
Chef	
Actor	
Politician	
Athlete	
Minister	
Businessperson	
Doctor	
Artist	
Musician	
Songwriter	
Teacher	
Other	

TIMOTHY'S TIME LINE

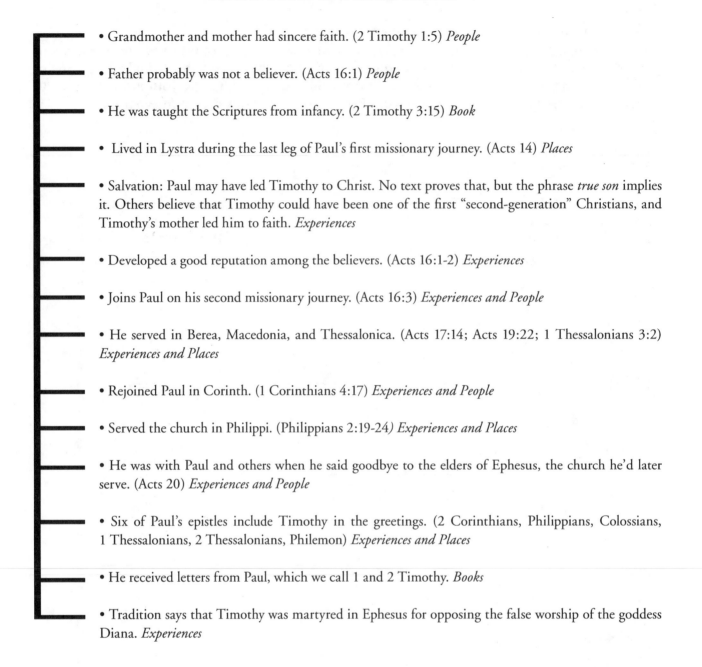

• Grandmother and mother had sincere faith. (2 Timothy 1:5) *People*

• Father probably was not a believer. (Acts 16:1) *People*

• He was taught the Scriptures from infancy. (2 Timothy 3:15) *Book*

• Lived in Lystra during the last leg of Paul's first missionary journey. (Acts 14) *Places*

• Salvation: Paul may have led Timothy to Christ. No text proves that, but the phrase *true son* implies it. Others believe that Timothy could have been one of the first "second-generation" Christians, and Timothy's mother led him to faith. *Experiences*

• Developed a good reputation among the believers. (Acts 16:1-2) *Experiences*

• Joins Paul on his second missionary journey. (Acts 16:3) *Experiences and People*

• He served in Berea, Macedonia, and Thessalonica. (Acts 17:14; Acts 19:22; 1 Thessalonians 3:2) *Experiences and Places*

• Rejoined Paul in Corinth. (1 Corinthians 4:17) *Experiences and People*

• Served the church in Philippi. (Philippians 2:19-24*) Experiences and Places*

• He was with Paul and others when he said goodbye to the elders of Ephesus, the church he'd later serve. (Acts 20) *Experiences and People*

• Six of Paul's epistles include Timothy in the greetings. (2 Corinthians, Philippians, Colossians, 1 Thessalonians, 2 Thessalonians, Philemon) *Experiences and Places*

• He received letters from Paul, which we call 1 and 2 Timothy. *Books*

• Tradition says that Timothy was martyred in Ephesus for opposing the false worship of the goddess Diana. *Experiences*

FOUR THINGS THAT CHANGED YOU

Fill in the following blanks.

1. Places you go
List four places that changed you:

_____

_____

_____

_____

2. People you know
List four people who've had the deepest impact on you:

_____

_____

_____

_____

3. Experiences that cause you to grow
Name four "mountaintop" experiences you've had:

_____

_____

_____

_____

Name four "valley" experiences you've had:

_____

_____

_____

_____

4. Books that cause you to grow
List four books that changed how you think:

_____

_____

_____

_____

JONATHAN EDWARDS' LEGACY
By Mark Merrill

Have you thought about your legacy lately? In case you haven't, let's start with the basics: Webster's Dictionary says a legacy is something handed down from one who has gone before.

Jonathan Edwards was born in 1703 in East Windsor, Connecticut. He attended Yale University at age 13 and later went on to serve as president of the College of New Jersey (now Princeton).

Edwards and his wife Sarah had 11 children. Despite a rigorous work schedule that included rising as early as 4:30 a.m. to read and write in his library, extensive travels, and endless administrative meetings, he always made time for his children. Indeed he committed to spending at least one hour a day with them. And what if he missed a day because he was traveling? He diligently made up the hour when he returned.

Numerous books have been written about Edwards' life, his work, his influence on American history, and his powerful professional legacy. But the legacy that Edwards would probably be most proud of is his legacy as a father.

The scholar Benjamin B. Warfield of Princeton has charted the 1,394 known descendents of Edwards. What he found was an incredible testament to Jonathan Edwards. Of his known descendents there were 13 college presidents, 65 college professors, 30 judges, 100 lawyers, 60 physicians, 75 army and navy officers, 100 pastors, 60 authors of prominence, 3 United States senators, 80 public servants in other capacities, including governors and ministers to foreign countries, and one vice president of the United States.

The story of Jonathan Edwards is an example of what some sociologists call the *five-generation rule*. How a parent raises their child—the love they give, the values they teach, the emotional environment they offer, the education they provide—influences not only their child, but also the four generations to follow. The example of Jonathan Edwards shows just how rich that legacy can be.

watch your leaders

WATCH FOR FALSE TEACHERS AND WATCH PAUL

session 2

During this session students will—

- Learn to distinguish between authentic faith and substitute faiths by knowing that God's Word is the standard for authenticity.
- Understand that we must use God-given guides to discern God's will.

■ THE BIG IDEA

Godly leaders in the church are gifts from God, but not every leader in the church is necessarily godly or from God.

■ BACKGROUND CHECK

Even though this letter is addressed to Timothy, it's intended to be read before the entire church in Ephesus. In part it served as a letter of recommendation for Timothy and his ministry. Timothy wasn't an apostle himself, but since the apostle Paul wrote this letter to him, it also served as an endorsement of Timothy, showing the church that Paul had chosen him to serve as his apostolic ambassador.

We're not exactly sure which falsehoods these teachers believed. Some people think it may have been a version of the Judaizers (those who wanted Gentile believers to obey the Jewish law in addition to experiencing grace through Christ Jesus in order to be *true believers*).

OPENING
Option 1: The Real Thing Challenge

You'll need—
- 2 volunteers
- 4 different types of soft drinks
- 2 blindfolds
- 10 cups

Ask for two volunteers. Since Coca-Cola® is the grandfather of all soft drinks, it is your standard. Blindfold the volunteers and have four different soft drinks for them to sample. However, you should have five cups per student because you need to include two cups of Coke® with your five drinks. Make the soft drinks Coca-Cola (two), Pepsi®, a generic cola, plus a non-cola (Mountain Dew Code Red® works well). See if they can name each soda simply by tasting it. (True connoisseurs might even be able to tell by smelling.)

After each student takes a drink ask, **Is that "The Real Thing"?** If they say no, ask them, **Which soft drink is it?**

If they say yes, ask them, **How do you know it's Coke?**

After each student has sampled all five cups, give the results of how well they did at guessing the soft drinks. Let them complete the contest before you give the results because you want to keep secret that two cups are the same (Coca-Cola).

After both students have tried to name the soft drinks, transition into the lesson by saying something along these lines—

They only knew which soft drink was "The Real Thing" because they've had Coke before. Now imagine if neither one of them had ever had a soft drink. Would they have been able to judge which soft drink was Coke? Only by having a standard are you able to know when something doesn't measure up. God has given us his standard of truth—the Bible. In the first chapter of 1 Timothy, he gives us an example of what a true leader or "the real thing" looks like— Paul, the author of 1 and 2 Timothy and Titus. So when Paul warns Timothy (and us) to beware of false leaders, we should pay attention.

Option 2: Do You Measure Up?

You'll need—
- 3 volunteers
- A 12-inch ruler or an 8.5 x 11-inch piece of paper (using 11 inches as the standard)

Get three students to stand in front of the group. Instruct them to raise their hands and put their palms together above their heads. Ask them to try to pull their hands apart exactly 12 inches—without looking up. Have the rest of the group vote on which person's hands they think are closest to 12 inches apart. Go behind them and use your ruler to measure the space between their hands.

Do it a second time but now let them lower their arms and put their hands in front of them before they do it. (If your group is small enough, let everyone try, and you can give away a small prize to whoever is closest.)

After you've determined who was closest to 12 inches, transition into the lesson by saying something along these lines—

One of them was closer to 12 inches than the others. We can only be sure of that because we had a 12-inch ruler to measure the space between their hands. Only by having a standard are you able to know when something doesn't measure up. God has given us his standard of truth—the Bible. In the first chapter of 1 Timothy, he gives us an example of what a true leader looks like—Paul, the author of 1 and 2 Timothy and Titus. So when Paul warns Timothy (and us) to beware of false leaders, we should pay attention.

READ IT IN GOD'S WORD
"Paul, an apostle of Christ Jesus by the command of God our Savior and of Christ Jesus our hope" (1 Timothy 1:1).

DID YOU KNOW?
WHAT'S AN APOSTLE?

Apostle literally means "one sent on a mission." In the broadest sense, every believer should be an apostle because we have been sent on a mission to share the gospel with the world. In the strictest sense, true apostles are those who saw Christ while he was on earth and those who were commissioned and sent out by him.

• Timothy knew Paul and his position. Paul's apostleship was mentioned so that the church people (including the false teachers with them) would know Paul had a special ministry that was equal to that of "The 12 Apostles." (Judas was no longer with them at this point, but Matthias had been chosen to replace him.)
• Paul never forgot that God saved him and desired people everywhere to be saved, too.

"To Timothy my true son in the faith: Grace, mercy and peace from God the Father and Christ Jesus our Lord" (1 Timothy 1:2).

• "True son in the faith" may hint at the fact that Paul personally led Timothy to faith in Christ. (There is no biblical reference that says that directly, but it's possible; some scholars believe it's probable.) Or it may just indicate that Timothy is such an example of the faith that he reminds Paul of himself.
• "Grace, mercy and peace"—Grace and peace were common greetings of the day. Peace is from the Hebrew word *shalom*, and grace emphasized the new covenant in Christ.
• Paul twice used mercy in his greetings to Timothy but never in his other epistles. It could be because ministry is so difficult that Paul felt that mercy is needed or because Paul wanted Timothy to have an extra dose of encouragement.

"As I urged you when I went into Macedonia, stay there in Ephesus so that you may command certain men not to teach false doctrines any longer" (1 Timothy 1:3).

• Paul and Timothy were together in Ephesus when Paul went to Macedonia. Paul didn't send Timothy to Ephesus; he left Timothy in Ephesus.
• "Stay there" may indicate that Timothy wanted to leave because of the difficulties in his church.
• From the very beginning of the letter we see the prominent theme—confronting false teachers—and its consequence on a body of believers or the church.

"... nor to devote themselves to myths and endless genealogies. These promote controversies rather than God's work—which is by faith" (1 Timothy 1:4).

• Instead of focusing on the things of God that were evident, these false teachers would teach or discuss things that God didn't mention or were not considered to be worth taking the time to talk about.

• If the teaching caused no harm, it might be bearable, but it was causing controversies within the church. These controversies took so much time to work through that the leaders could not devote their time to doing what they were supposed to do, which was God's work.

"The goal of this command is love, which comes from a pure heart and a good conscience and a sincere faith" (1 Timothy 1:5).

• Timothy's goal is love. Followers of Jesus need to believe the right things, but how you live should match your beliefs, and love should be your driving force.

• Jesus told us we should, "'Love the Lord your God with all your heart and with all your soul and with all your strength and with all your mind'; and, 'Love your neighbor as yourself.'" (Luke 10:27)

DID YOU KNOW?
WHAT'S YOUR MOTTO?

Mission Year is a mission organization that coordinates teams of six who live, volunteer, and worship in one inner city community for one year, serving the poor in the name of Jesus. Their motto is simple and direct: "Love God. Love People. Nothing Else Matters." That would be a good motto for all of us to memorize and live.

"Some have wandered away from these and turned to meaningless talk. They want to be teachers of the law, but they do not know what they are talking about or what they so confidently affirm" (1 Timothy 1:6-7).

• Leadership is more about who you are than what you do. Through all their meaningless talk, they showed they didn't have the character to be biblical leaders.

ACTIVITY
DIFFERENT CHURCHES—SAME PROBLEMS

You'll need—
• Copies of **Different Churches—Same Problems** (page 26) for each student
• Pen or pencil for each student

Hand out the **Different Churches—Same Problems** (page 26) and have the students work on the questions individually for about five minutes. Then briefly discuss their responses to the questions. Both churches referred to in 1 Timothy and Titus have problems! This activity could be a good starting place for a discussion about issues like unity in your own church or youth group.

"We know that the law is good if one uses it properly" (1 Timothy 1:8).

• How is the law used properly? Paul is about to tell us.

"We also know that law is made not for the righteous but for lawbreakers and rebels, the ungodly and sinful, the unholy and irreligious; for those who kill their fathers or mothers, for murderers, for adulterers and perverts, for slave traders and liars and perjurers—and for whatever else is contrary to the sound doctrine that conforms to the glorious gospel of the blessed God, which he entrusted to me" (1 Timothy 1:9-11).

• Did you see anything familiar in the verses we just read? Read them again.

"I thank Christ Jesus our Lord, who has given me strength, that he considered me faithful, appointing me to his service" (1 Timothy 1:12).

• Paul focuses on where he was as a part of humanity against God. After he reflects on this, he begins to thank God for everything he had done for him. We are faithful because of what God can do through us, not because of what we can do for God.
• God will give you the strength to do whatever he wants you to do.

"Even though I was once a blasphemer and a persecutor and a violent man, I was shown mercy because I acted in ignorance and unbelief" (1 Timothy 1:13).

• Paul never forgot what he was like before he encountered Christ. He was a Pharisee, a persecutor of The Way—sinful despite believing the right things.

"The grace of our Lord was poured out on me abundantly, along with the faith and love that are in Christ Jesus. Here is a trustworthy saying that deserves full acceptance: Christ Jesus came into the world to save sinners—of whom I am the worst" (1 Timothy 1:14-15).

• The reason for the concern about the false teachers and the end result of God's love is the offer of salvation, because Jesus came into the world to save sinners.
• "Christ Jesus came into the world to save sinners—of whom I am the worst"—The older you get the more you realize how great is the distance between your good works and God's perfect standard.

"But for that very reason I was shown mercy so that in me, the worst of sinners, Christ Jesus might display his unlimited patience as an example for those who would believe on him and receive eternal life" (1 Timothy 1:16).

• Paul is just trying to say, "If God can save and use me, he can save and use anybody."

"Now to the King eternal, immortal, invisible, the only God, be honor and glory forever and ever. Amen" (1 Timothy 1:17).

• The more you learn about God—like how great he is and all that he has offered to us—the better you will praise and worship him.

LIVE IT IN YOUR WORLD

If Paul and Timothy had fights within their church, don't be discouraged when it happens to you. We also need to learn when something is important enough to argue about and when it's okay to let it go.

ACTIVITY
FIGHT ABOUT IT OR LET IT GO?

You'll need—
• Copies of **Fight About It or Let It Go?** (page 29) for each student
• Pen or pencil for each student

Hand out copies of **Fight About It or Let It Go?** (page 29). Begin by saying something like—

No one's beliefs are perfect because we are limited people trying to understand an unlimited God. There are some things that should be vitally important (non-negotiable beliefs) and other things that are not as important (negotiable beliefs). And some things are "it-doesn't-matter" beliefs, while others are wrong beliefs.

Let's take a look at this worksheet that will help us figure out where we stand on some issues that can divide people from different religious backgrounds, as well as people in the same church.

Ask for a show of hands among your students to see where their beliefs fall between non-negotiable beliefs and wrong beliefs. (This will also give you a better idea of what topics you may need to cover during future lessons.) Encourage any discussion that may result from this survey.

PUT IT IN YOUR HEART

"Here is a trustworthy saying that deserves full acceptance: Christ Jesus came into the world to save sinners—of whom I am the worst" (1 Timothy 1:15) .

SMALL GROUP QUESTIONS

1. What are the benefits of staying and working through a problem instead of running from it?
2. Are there any problems in your life right now? Are you staying and working on them or do you want to run from them?
3. How much of what you see being done for God seems to lack God? Why do you think that is? How can you do things differently?
4. What are some ways that truth or the idea of truth is challenged today?
5. What are some things people put their hope in?
6. Which one are you more likely to have—a pure heart, a good conscience, or a sincere faith? Why aren't the other areas stronger? What are you willing to do to become strong in all three?
7. What are some current controversial issues in the news?
8. What are some current controversial issues in the Church (not just your local congregation)?
9. Are there any current controversial issues in your local congregation?
10. What percentage of your daily schedule is done out of love?

CLOSING PRAYER

DIFFERENT CHURCHES—SAME PROBLEMS

"As I urged you when I went into Macedonia, stay there in Ephesus so that you may command certain men not to teach false doctrines any longer, nor to devote themselves to myths and endless genealogies. These promote controversies rather than God's work—which is by faith. The goal of this command is love, which comes from a pure heart and a good conscience and a sincere faith. Some have wandered away from these and turned to meaningless talk. They want to be teachers of the law, but they do not know what they are talking about or what they so confidently affirm" (1 Timothy 1:3-7).

"But avoid foolish controversies and genealogies and arguments and quarrels about the law, because these are unprofitable and useless. Warn a divisive person once, and then warn him a second time. After that, have nothing to do with him. You may be sure that such a man is warped and sinful; he is self-condemned" (Titus 3:9-11).

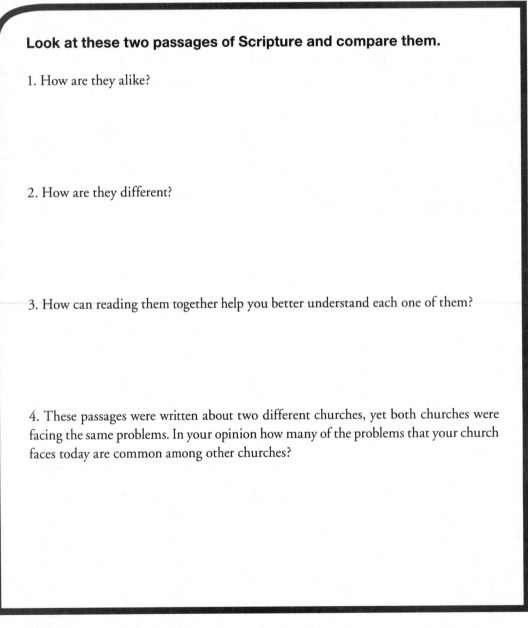

Look at these two passages of Scripture and compare them.

1. How are they alike?

2. How are they different?

3. How can reading them together help you better understand each one of them?

4. These passages were written about two different churches, yet both churches were facing the same problems. In your opinion how many of the problems that your church faces today are common among other churches?

DID YOU SEE IT?

"We also know that law is made not for the righteous but for lawbreakers and rebels, the ungodly and sinful, the unholy and irreligious; for those who kill their fathers or mothers, for murderers, for adulterers and perverts, for slave traders and liars and perjurers—and for whatever else is contrary to the sound doctrine that conforms to the glorious gospel of the blessed God, which he entrusted to me" (1 Timothy 1:9-11).

The false teachers of the law didn't understand the law. Paul's list paralleled the Ten Commandments—the Jewish readers of that day would have seen it automatically. Look at the list below and determine how many of these commandments you've broken, especially in your heart (where Jesus puts the focus).

1. Lawbreakers and Rebels
First commandment: "You shall have no other gods before me" (Exodus 20:3).
What's the most important thing in your life? What do you think about when you have nothing to think about? That may be your god.

2. Ungodly and Sinful
Third commandment: "You shall not misuse the name of the Lord your God" (Exodus 20:7).
This is more than just saying a swear word or phrase. It also means wearing the Christian label (calling yourself a Christian) but not living like a Christian should. If you do that, you've taken God's name in vain.

3. Unholy and Irreligious (Irreligious means they would not honor any day as holy.)
Fourth commandment: "Remember the Sabbath day by keeping it holy" (Exodus 20:8).
We don't have to observe the Sabbath in the same way that Israel did; but we should rest regularly, which is a Christian commitment based upon the order of creation. And we are told in Hebrews 10:25 that we should not neglect meeting together.

4. Those Who Kill Their Fathers or Mothers (the ultimate act of not honoring your parents)
Fifth commandment: "Honor your father and your mother" (Exodus 20:12).
Do you honor your parents daily? Do you respect their views even if you don't agree with them?

5. Murderers
Sixth commandment: "You shall not murder" (Exodus 20:13).
We are probably safe on this one except for what Jesus says, "You have heard that it was said to the people long ago, 'Do not murder, and anyone who murders will be subject to judgment.' But I tell you that anyone who is angry with his brother will be subject to judgment" (Matthew 5:21-22).

From Creative Bible Lessons in 1 & 2 Timothy and Titus by Len Evans. Permission to reproduce this page granted only for use in buyer's own youth group. ©2004 by Youth Specialties. www.YouthSpecialties.com

6. Adulterers and Perverts

Seventh commandment: "You shall not commit adultery" (Exodus 20:14).

Any sort of sexual gratification outside of God's design is wrong: "But I tell you that anyone who looks at a woman lustfully has already committed adultery with her in his heart" (Matthew 5:28).

7. Slave Traders
(Paul was thinking of kidnappers; the ultimate act of stealing is to steal a person.)

Eighth commandment: "You shall not steal" (Exodus 20:15).

Ever shoplift a little thing from a store? Ever steal an answer from a test? Ever download music from the Internet illegally? Ever rob a bank? Whether big or little, it's stealing, and it displeases God.

8. Liars and Perjurers

Ninth commandment: "You shall not give false testimony against your neighbor" (Exodus 20:16).

9. Whatever else is contrary to the sound doctrine

FIGHT ABOUT IT OR LET IT GO?

Label the statements below with the letter that most closely indicates where you stand on each issue.

A. Non-negotiable Belief
B. Negotiable Belief
C. "It-Doesn't-Matter" Belief
D. Wrong Belief

_____ The virgin birth

_____ Grape juice only for communion

_____ Mary was always a virgin

_____ God created the world in seven days

_____ Jesus will establish a 1,000-year kingdom

_____ Christians should read their Bible every day

_____ Salvation is totally free

_____ Coke is better than Pepsi

_____ Communion should be done weekly

_____ Christians should agree with other faiths

_____ Denominations are totally wrong

_____ Speaking in tongues

_____ Jesus is the only way to Heaven

_____ All the books in the Bible are from God

_____ Jesus will return

_____ Baptism

_____ Christians shouldn't drive SUVs

_____ Christians should be sensitive to other faiths

_____ Buddha spoke some truth

_____ Jesus came back to life with a physical body

_____ Christians should be active in a church

_____ All truth is God's truth

watch your worship

WORSHIP IS WHAT IT'S ALL ABOUT!

session 3

During this session students will—

- Realize that prayer is a vital component of our everyday faith.
- Wrestle with a difficult passage involving worship and women in the Ephesus church.

■ THE BIG IDEA

Worship is not a Sunday-morning appointment but an everyday attitude.

■ BACKGROUND CHECK

This chapter contains one of the most controversial passages in the New Testament and one of the most difficult verses to understand and interpret in the entire Bible! This is the sort of writing that Peter must have had in mind when he writes about Paul, "His letters contain some things that are hard to understand" (2 Peter 3:16).

OPENING

Option 1: Mostly True

You'll need—
- Blank sheet of paper for each participant
- Pen or pencil for each participant

First decide if you want students to break off into smaller groups to do this activity, or just choose a few students (and possibly adult leaders) to do it for the whole group. Then give the participants paper, something to write with, and a few minutes to think about what they're going to write.

The object is to reveal unknown things about yourself in a fun atmosphere. The people who are playing the game should write down four things about themselves. Three must be true statements and one should be false. For example: "I'm a Boston Red Sox fan. I have been to Haiti. I have an Aunt Marcia. I took ballet for three years."

Each person reads his answers, and the group tries to guess which statement is false. If you want to keep score, a correct guess about someone else's false statement earns a player one point, but if the group fails to identify the lie, then the person who's sharing earns five points. Each person should get a chance to share.

After everyone has spoken, say—

I have one more name to introduce for our game. It is worship. Which of the following statements is not true about worship?

> *1. Men and women can both worship God.*
> *2. You have to be in a church building to worship.*
> *3. Worship involves more than singing.*
> *4. Prayer is vital to worship.*

Give the students a chance to guess. Then transition with something like this—

There are a lot of misconceptions about worship and—as crazy as it sounds—people in churches even fight over worship and worship styles.

Today we're going to look at some guidelines that Paul gave to Timothy about worship for men and women, prayer for everyone, and how he wrote that worship is a lifestyle.

Option 2: Controversial Church-Quakes!

You'll need—
- Copies of **Controversial Church-Quakes!** (pages 37-38) for each student
- Pen or pencil for each student

Pass out copies of **Controversial Church-Quakes!** (pages 37-38) and something to write with. Go over the six ratings on the number lines to make sure your students understand what each one means, then give them some time to complete the repro page. Once everyone is finished, discuss some of the differences and see (maybe by a show of hands) where your students fall on the Theological Richter Scale.

Then transition with something like this—

There have always been fights and disputes among Christians. There are a lot of misconceptions about worship and—as crazy as it sounds—people in churches even fight over worship and worship styles.

Today we're going to look at some guidelines that Paul gave to Timothy about worship for men and women, prayer for everyone, and how he wrote that worship is a lifestyle.

READ IT IN GOD'S WORD

"I urge, then, first of all, that requests, prayers, intercession and thanksgiving be made for everyone" (1 Timothy 2:1).

• Urge is the same word Paul used to encourage Timothy to remain in Ephesus; then he refers back to all of chapter 1. As you may remember, the theme of chapter 1 talked about false teachers and Paul being the true teacher. The context of the false teachers influences most of this letter to Timothy.
• In light of the false teachers, Paul gives his first prescription to maintain healthy worship—prayer!
• There are seven different words used in the New Testament regarding prayer, and we have four of them in this one verse.
• Praying for everyone doesn't mean that your phone book needs to become your prayer book. The implication is that we should be praying for people of all ages, nationalities, races, and backgrounds.
• Intercession is the same as the idea we read about in Hebrews 4:16: "So whenever we are in need, we should come bravely before the throne of our merciful God" (CEV). As believers who have been adopted by God, we don't need an appointment to see the King; we can approach him with confidence because we are his children!

"For kings and all those in authority, that we may live peaceful and quiet lives in all godliness and holiness" (1 Timothy 2:2).

• According to Romans 13:1-5, everyone is under someone's authority, and God wants us to pray for our leaders. We could apply this by praying for our national, state, and local leaders.
• We are to pray for our national leader(s) whether we voted for them or not.
• Godliness is used 10 times in 13 chapters of the Pastoral Epistles. (This is a theme we will cover in more detail later.)

"This is good, and pleases God our Savior" (1 Timothy 2:3).

• Our ultimate aim in life is to please God in all that we do. Whenever we do God's will, it pleases God.

"...who wants all men to be saved and to come to a knowledge of the truth" (1 Timothy 2:4).

• No one is beyond God's reach. We should pray even for the person who we think is the *least likely* to become a Christian.

ILLUSTRATION OPTION
REAL LIFE—LIFE CHANGE

Jeffrey Dahmer was one of the most horrific men in recent memory. Dahmer was a serial killer who abducted, raped, tortured, murdered, and cannibalized his victims. He claimed to have had a conversion experience and become a Christian before he was beaten and killed on November 28, 1994.

"I always believed the theory of evolution as truth, that we all just came from the slime. When we—when we died, you know, that was it, there is nothing, and I've since come to believe that the Lord Jesus Christ is truly God, and I believe that I, as well as everyone else, will be accountable to him." —Jeffrey Dahmer (*Dateline NBC*: "The Final Interview," broadcast on November 29, 1994)

Did Dahmer proclaim faith to get more media attention, or did he truly become a Christian? We won't know for sure until we are in Heaven. Would it be impossible for God to save Dahmer?

ACTIVITY
PRAYING FOR MY TOP 10

You'll need—
• Copies of **Praying for My Top 10** (page 39)
• Pen or pencil for each student

Before the lesson, copy the **Praying for My Top 10** (page 39) and cut apart the prayer bookmarks for the students to use as they pray for different people.

Pass out the bookmarks and something to write with to each student. Instruct them to write down the names of 10 people they want to begin praying for regularly. Tell them—

You can put any names on the bookmark that you wish, but in light of Paul encouraging us to pray for everyone and our leaders, here is a suggestion: Write down the names of three friends, two national leaders, two family members, one famous person, one world leader, and one group of Christians living in a "closed" country.

OPTIONAL ACTIVITY
MORE PRAYER INSIGHTS

You'll need—
• Two-sided copies of **Prayer Web Sites** and **Prayer Quotes** (pages 40-41), one for each student

Pass out copies of the **Prayer Web Sites/Prayer Quotes** handouts (pages 40-41). Point out the listing of Web sites for students to check out on their own time. Then ask them to look at the quotes about prayer. Ask them to read through the quotes and note which one(s) they identify with the best. Then ask a few students to share what they like about the quote they chose.

"For there is one God and one mediator between God and men, the man Christ Jesus" (1 Timothy 2:5).

• In the ancient world as today, people believed there were many ways to get to Heaven and many gods. But a cornerstone of the Jewish faith, which Jesus also referred to, is, "Hear, O Israel: The Lord our God, the Lord is one" (Deuteronomy 6:4).
• Jesus is the only mediator between God and man, and he's the only one who ever could fill that role because he is fully God and fully man!

"...who gave himself as a ransom for all men—the testimony given in its proper time" (1 Timothy 2:6).

• Ransom refers to the price paid to redeem a slave or a prisoner. The ransom was not paid to Satan. Mankind owes the debt to God because we failed to meet his standard of perfection apart from Christ. Christ paid the price for us—that's the testimony that was given to us at the proper time.

"And for this purpose I was appointed a herald and an apostle—I am telling the truth, I am not lying—and a teacher of the true faith to the Gentiles" (1 Timothy 2:7).

• Context demands that Paul is contrasting himself—the true teacher—to the false teachers that are referred to in this book.
• Paul reminds us that God still wants to save everyone, not just the Jews (Gentiles, too).
• *Herald* shows that Paul was a messenger of the Good News, specifically to the Gentiles.

"I want men everywhere to lift up holy hands in prayer, without anger or disputing" (1 Timothy 2:8).

• This is the pivot verse for this section. The verses before this one pertain to prayer and the verses after it refer to the roles of men and women in the church. This verse deals with prayer and the role of men in the church.
• The important part is not to have your hands lifted high when you pray but rather to lift holy hands when you pray! (Psalm 24:3-4)
• Lifting up your hands was and is a common expression of worship. It is an act of openness and willingness to follow God wherever he wants people to go.
• It's important to note that Paul refers to men here and not just church leaders.

"I also want women to dress modestly, with decency and propriety, not with braided hair or gold or pearls or expensive clothes, but with good deeds, appropriate for women who profess to worship God" (1 Timothy 2:9-10).

• Paul had just mentioned men specifically, so it shouldn't be surprising that he would then mention women specifically.
• Modesty and motives matter. The important issue is that we clothe ourselves with righteousness and reverence rather than riches.
• Is it wrong for women to have their hair braided? These well-described styles that Paul mentions were the norm for the prostitutes who worked in the temples of Diana in Ephesus. So these instructions seem aimed more at the culture than at Christians.
• "Expensive clothes" at that time meant an outfit worth almost a year's salary. Rather than instructing women to wear rags, Paul is actually warning against extravagance.
• Paul is encouraging women to dress modestly so as not to take attention away from God.
• Peter says something similar to women when he writes, "Instead, [a woman's beauty] should be that of your inner self, the unfading beauty of a gentle and quiet spirit, which is of great worth in God's sight" (1 Peter 3:3-4).

(CAUTION! These next few verses are controversial, but we're going to look at them anyway. Why? Because all Scripture is God breathed and is useful for us—even the parts that aren't the easiest to understand or explain. Use your judgment and consult with your pastor before getting into this section with your students!)

"A woman should learn in quietness and full submission. I do not permit a woman to teach or to have authority over a man; she must be silent" (1 Timothy 2:11-12).

• This is one of the most disputed sections in the New Testament! An important thing to remember while you look at this passage is that God desires order in our worship (1 Corinthians 14:26-40).

OPTIONAL ACTIVITY
DEBATE

Arrange for a debate—real or staged—between two or three people (students or leaders) regarding the roles of women in the church. Give the participants enough advance notice so they can do their research and fully prepare their arguments ahead of time. Or you could use this time to explain to the students what your church (or tradition) teaches about the role of women in the church.

- Ask students to share their reactions to this passage.
- Explain the four basic views of this passage and how Christians today differ on the role of women in ministry—

1. Weaker gender view: This view says women should remain silent in church, and they should never teach men because they are the weaker gender.
2. Headship view: This view says men and women have different roles based upon their gender, but both have equal value in God's sight.
3. Spiritual gifts view: This view says women and men can do anything in the church if they have the appropriate spiritual gifts.
4. Egalitarian view: This view says women and men are totally equal, and there are no limits to what women can do within the church.

- Ask—**Which view makes the most sense to you? What other verses or passages in the Bible cause you to believe that way?**

- The Greek word *hasychia* is translated as "quietness" in verse 11 but "silent" in verse 12. There is a different word (*siga*) that is used to mean "to be silent, to say nothing." So if Paul wanted women to always be mute in church services for all time, he would have used the word *siga*. He didn't. So how does that affect the way we interpret this passage?
- Before we get too emotional over this issue, the first thing we should realize is that women were encouraged to learn in the church. This stance was against the cultural norms of that time.

"For Adam was formed first, then Eve. And Adam was not the one deceived; it was the woman who was deceived and became a sinner" (1 Timothy 2:13-14).

- The snake did not deceive Adam, but he still sinned. Is Adam guilty, or is Eve guilty, or are both of them guilty?

"But women will be saved through childbearing—if they continue in faith, love and holiness with propriety" (1 Timothy 2:15).

- Does giving birth to children save women? If so, how are men saved? Or what about women who never give birth?
- The word *saved* literally has more to do with the idea of being preserved rather than having a direct correlation with spiritual salvation. Does it mean that a believing woman is preserved through the painful act of giving birth?
- Others suggest it might mean that a believing woman will primarily find her purpose in being preserved for raising a family.
- Still others say it refers to Mary giving birth to Jesus, which enabled him to come to Earth and offer salvation to everyone.

LIVE IT IN YOUR WORLD
Live the life of worship in everything you do.

QUOTE
"There are not three levels of spiritual life—worship, waiting, and work. Yet some of us seem to jump like spiritual frogs from worship to waiting and from waiting to work. God's idea is that the three should go together as one. They were always together in the life of our Lord and in perfect harmony. It is a discipline that must be developed; it will not happen overnight."
—Oswald Chambers in *My Utmost for His Highest*

PUT IT IN YOUR HEART

"For there is one God and one mediator between God and men, the man Christ Jesus" (1 Timothy 2:5).

SMALL GROUP QUESTIONS

1. In what ways is prayer easy for you?
2. In what ways is prayer difficult for you?
3. Is it difficult for you to pray out loud? Explain.
4. How often do you pray?
5. What are different ways we can pray?
6. How would you rate your prayers?
7. How do you know if your prayers have been answered?
8. Do you really believe that God can save anybody?
9. In your opinion who are the top three people who can't be saved? Are you willing to start praying for them?
10. What are different ways we can worship?
11. How should worship be a lifestyle?
12. Do you think men and women are different? Explain.
13. Does God treat men and women differently? Explain.
14. Is it wrong today for women to wear braided hair?

ACTIVITY
OPTIONAL CLOSING IDEA

If you're able to, darken your meeting room and only use candles, lava lamps, or even Christmas lights for illumination. Say something like this—

Today we are going to close in prayer a little differently. We just talked about worship, so now I'd like you to go before God and ask him to make you a better worshiper and to show you what you need to do. After a time of silence I'm going to play a worship song*, and I invite you to make it your prayer.

After the song say, "Amen."

* NOTE: A song that works well is "O Praise Him" (All This for a King) by the David Crowder Band.

CLOSING PRAYER

CONTROVERSIAL CHURCH-QUAKES!

Christians argue with other Christians about many things that are not necessarily salvation issues. Would you be willing to fight over these theological issues? Where do they rank on the Theological Richter Scale? Circle your response on each number line below.

0.0 – Doesn't even register with you. *(It doesn't matter what a person believes on this one.)*

2.0 – The experts know something occurred, but no one else does. *(There are differences, but it's not a big issue.)*

4.0 - A little shake but life goes on normally. *(These are differences I can live with.)*

6.0 – Everyone talks about it the next day. *(You feel a little uncomfortable if someone disagrees with you.)*

8.0 – You're afraid you might get hurt or die. *(You are willing to risk a lot over this issue because you know you're right.)*

10.0 – There's no escape! *(If someone else believes differently than you, then he is a heretic and you'll fight to the death over this issue!)*

1. Baptism

| 0.0 | 2.0 | 4.0 | 6.0 | 8.0 | 10.0 |

Some churches only baptize adults; others baptize babies and children. A few churches believe baptism is necessary for salvation. Most believe baptism is a vital expression of our faith but not necessary for salvation. And a few churches don't make a big deal out of baptism. Some sprinkle water, others pour water, others immerse people in water, and one time a church had a mass baptism and used a fire hose!

2. Worship Styles

| 0.0 | 2.0 | 4.0 | 6.0 | 8.0 | 10.0 |

Churches in the English-speaking world have a wide variety of worship styles and worship services that are labeled "Christian." Some sing only hymns, others use only contemporary praise and worship songs, and others combine those two styles. Some churches use candles and incense, others use PowerPoint slides, and still others would never use PowerPoint. Some sermons are 45 to 50 minutes long, while others would never go over 20 minutes.

3. Communion

| 0.0 | 2.0 | 4.0 | 6.0 | 8.0 | 10.0 |

Some churches celebrate The Lord's Supper every week, others once a month. Some churches use wine, others only use grape juice. Some think something spiritual happens, and others think it's merely a physical act of remembrance. Some churches require their clergy to bless the bread and wine or juice, while others maintain that any believer can offer communion to other believers.

4. End Times   0.0   2.0   4.0   6.0   8.0   10.0

Jesus will return physically in the future. Jesus has already returned spiritually. Some believe there is no rapture; some say the rapture will happen before the tribulation; others say in the middle of the tribulation, and still others say at the end of the tribulation.

5. Spiritual Gifts   0.0   2.0   4.0   6.0   8.0   10.0

There are churches that believe some spiritual gifts are no longer relevant today; others believe that every spiritual gift listed in the New Testament is still necessary and used today. And others add some spiritual gifts from the Old Testament to either one of those lists.

6. Women in Ministry   0.0   2.0   4.0   6.0   8.0   10.0

Some churches say women are totally equal with men—both in their value and their role in the church. Some believe women shouldn't cut their hair, wear makeup, or teach men, and they have other rules like these that are for women only. Some believe that women can do anything based upon their spiritual gifts, whatever they may be. Others believe that women are equal with men in value but not in their role.

PRAYING FOR MY TOP 10

I URGE, THEN, FIRST OF ALL, THAT REQUESTS, PRAYERS, INTERCESSION AND THANKSGIVING BE MADE FOR EVERYONE (1 TIMOTHY 2:1).

1. _____
   _____
2. _____
   _____
3. _____
   _____
4. _____
   _____
5. _____
   _____
6. _____
   _____
7. _____
   _____
8. _____
   _____
9. _____
   _____
10. _____
    _____

THIS IS GOOD, AND PLEASES GOD OUR SAVIOR, WHO WANTS ALL MEN TO BE SAVED AND TO COME TO A KNOWLEDGE OF THE TRUTH (1 TIMOTHY 2:3-4).

I URGE, THEN, FIRST OF ALL, THAT REQUESTS, PRAYERS, INTERCESSION AND THANKSGIVING BE MADE FOR EVERYONE (1 TIMOTHY 2:1).

1. _____
   _____
2. _____
   _____
3. _____
   _____
4. _____
   _____
5. _____
   _____
6. _____
   _____
7. _____
   _____
8. _____
   _____
9. _____
   _____
10. _____
    _____

THIS IS GOOD, AND PLEASES GOD OUR SAVIOR, WHO WANTS ALL MEN TO BE SAVED AND TO COME TO A KNOWLEDGE OF THE TRUTH (1 TIMOTHY 2:3-4).

I URGE, THEN, FIRST OF ALL, THAT REQUESTS, PRAYERS, INTERCESSION AND THANKSGIVING BE MADE FOR EVERYONE (1 TIMOTHY 2:1).

1. _____
   _____
2. _____
   _____
3. _____
   _____
4. _____
   _____
5. _____
   _____
6. _____
   _____
7. _____
   _____
8. _____
   _____
9. _____
   _____
10. _____
    _____

THIS IS GOOD, AND PLEASES GOD OUR SAVIOR, WHO WANTS ALL MEN TO BE SAVED AND TO COME TO A KNOWLEDGE OF THE TRUTH (1 TIMOTHY 2:3-4).

PRAYER WEB SITES

http://www.gmi.org/ow/
Operation World: Learn how to pray for a different country each day of the year.

http://www.basicfellowship.com
Voice of the Martyrs: Learn more about the how the church around the world is persecuted and what you can do to help through prayer and by putting your prayers into action.

http://www.praymag.com
Pray! magazine: an online magazine about prayer.

http://www.nationalprayer.org/
National Prayer Committee: a diverse group of men and women who feel God's calling to help lead the prayer movement in America. The Web site contains information about their various prayer ministries and events, as well as updates and stories about how God is working in America.

http://www.presidentialprayerteam.org
Presidential Prayer Team: The independent, nonprofit organization behind The Presidential Prayer Team has a singular purpose: to encourage specific nationwide prayer for the President. The goal is to enlist at least 2.8 million participants, or one percent of the American population, to make this prayer commitment.

http://www.centeringprayer.com/lectio.htm
Lectio Divina: an ancient way of prayer that has regained a lot of attention and devotion among Christians around the world in recent years.

http://www.methodx.net/
MethodX: (the way of Christ) is an online Christian community where young adults (college to 30s) can identify and explore their relationships with God and with others. It is sponsored by Upper Room Ministries®, an interdenominational, global Christian ministry.

http://www.billbright.com/howtofast/
Your Personal Guide to Fasting and Prayer by Bill Bright. "Fasting is the most powerful spiritual discipline of all the Christian disciplines. Through fasting and prayer, the Holy Spirit can transform your life."

http://www.sacredgateway.org
Sacred Gateway: a guided session of prayer in six different stages.

PRAYER QUOTES

Which of the following quotes about prayer do you most identify with?

"Prayer honors God; it dishonors self. It is man's plea of weakness, ignorance, want; a plea which heaven cannot disregard. God delights to have us pray." —E. M. Bounds

"Do not pray for easy lives. Pray to be stronger men and women. Do not pray for tasks equal to your powers. Pray for powers equal to your tasks." —Phillips Brooks

"The one concern of the devil is to keep Christians from praying. He fears nothing from prayerless studies, prayerless work and prayerless religion. He laughs at our toil, mocks at our wisdom, but trembles when we pray." —Samuel Chadwick

"Every great movement of God can be traced to a kneeling figure." —D. L. Moody

"Prayer is a grace through which we pour ourselves out before God and through which He calls us into His presence. If it is anything other than that, it is not prayer—it is the practice of magic." —Rich Mullins

"The condition of the church may be very accurately gauged by its prayer meetings. So is the prayer meeting a graceometer, and from it we may judge the amount of divine working among a people. If God be near a church, it must pray. And if he be not there, one of the first tokens of his absence will be a slothfulness in prayer." —Charles Haddon Spurgeon

"Pray for great things, expect great things, work for great things, but above all, pray." —R. A. Torrey

prepare to lead

IT'S A CHARACTER ISSUE!

session 4

During this session students will—

- Realize that before you are given a position of leadership, you must become a person worthy of leadership.
- Understand that in order to progress in their own spiritual maturity, they need to have a plan to grow within a community of believers.
- Be encouraged to view their faith in a holistic manner and not categorize different areas of their lives.

■ THE BIG IDEA

Leadership is about being the person you are, not the position you have. Leaders in a church must have the highest character.

■ BACKGROUND CHECK

Churches, regardless of their particular flavor of church government or structure will use this chapter to defend their position. The Pastoral Epistles are sometimes held up as a *rule book* for churches and ministry. While the Pastoral Epistles do give us good principles and truths for our churches and how to do ministry, these books were never intended to be the "be all and end all" guidebook for churches.

Paul wanted the church in Ephesus to follow the instructions he gave to Timothy. Our churches should follow them, too. However, since it's extremely rare for a student to be the point person for an entire church, we are going to focus on the general principles that flow out of the specific prescription from Paul.

OPENING
Option 1: Trustworthy Leadership Sayings

You'll need—
- Double-sided copies of **Trustworthy Leadership Sayings** and **What Do You Look for in a Leader?** (pages 48-49) for each student
- Pen or pencil for each student

Pass out the list of Trustworthy Leadership Sayings (page 48) along with something to write with and instruct your students to circle the four sayings they like the best. Then ask the students to share their choices. (You could also divide students into smaller groups of two to four and have them share their four choices and why they preferred them in that setting.)

If your students aren't already split up into smaller groups, divide them up now. Ask students to go to the repro page, **What Do You Look for in a Leader?** (p. 49). Introduce this activity by saying something like this—

I'd like you to think of some great leaders. They could be political leaders, military leaders, religious leaders, or any other person you consider to be a leader. Work together in your discussion groups and come up with the answers to these four questions on your sheets.

The directives your students will be considering are—
1. List the three greatest leaders of the past 100 years.
2. List three things about each leader that made or makes him great.
3. List the three greatest leaders of all time.
4. List three things about each leader (from your list in question three) that made or makes her great.

Ask a few groups to share their responses. Then choose a student to read aloud 1 Samuel 16:7: "The Lord does not look at the things man looks at. Man looks at the outward appearance, but the Lord looks at the heart."

Option 2: Movie Clip
The Patriot

You'll need—
- *The Patriot* (Columbia Pictures, 2000)
- TV and DVD player

Start 01:06:25. The reverend is standing in the pulpit, and the people are singing. Martin walks through the door of the church to make an announcement.

Stop 01:10:25, The newly formed militia rides off.

In this scene from *The Patriot*, Gabriel Martin (Heath Ledger) goes into the church to try to recruit some fighters for the South Carolina militia. Many of the men are reluctant to follow him at first because the Red Coats aren't afraid to hang anyone who resists their rule over the colonies.

After the clip is over, start a discussion with the following questions—

- Anne Howard says, "Will you now, when you are needed most, stop at only words? Is that the sort of men you

are? I ask only that you act upon the beliefs of which you have so strongly spoken and in which you so strongly believe." What truths do you see in Anne's challenge to the men in her church?
• What could be different in your life if you acted upon what you believed more often?
• Mr. Howard is shocked when he sees the reverend walk away with a rifle in his hand. But the reverend responds, "The shepherd must tend his flock and at times fight off the wolves!" Is that the kind of pastor or leader you'd like to have? Why or why not?
• Does the reverend's statement reflect biblical truth?

Encourage them for their participation and transition into the lesson with something like—

The reverend put his faith into action and sought to protect his congregation literally and symbolically by going to fight for them. Leaders have to stand up and fight off people and false ideas that could harm the flock that God has given to them.

In chapter 3 of 1 Timothy, Paul offers some guidance about how to choose leaders in the church and how to be a leader in the church.

READ IT IN GOD'S WORD

"Here is a trustworthy saying: If anyone sets his heart on being an overseer, he desires a noble task" (1 Timothy 3:1).

• It's okay to desire a position of leadership as long as you realize that you are going to serve others—they will not serve you.

"Now the overseer must be above reproach, the husband of but one wife, temperate, self-controlled, respectable, hospitable, able to teach" (1 Timothy 3:2).

ACTIVITY
COMPARE AND CONTRAST

You'll need—
• Double-sided copies of **Compare and Contrast** and **Biblical Leadership Traits** (pages 50-51) for each student
• Pen or pencil for each student
• Bibles

You may want students to pair off for this activity. Hand out copies of **Compare and Contrast/Biblical Leadership Traits** (pages 50-51) and something to write with. Make sure students have access to a Bible so they can compare the two passages referred to on one side of the repro page. Give them five minutes to work on their comparisons and then discuss their findings.

Next ask them to work individually to rank the importance of each leadership quality. Give them a few more minutes to complete this side of the handout. Ask for a show of hands to see if anyone rated one of the traits a "10." Ask which traits received a "0" score. Choose a few students to share which traits received the highest ranking on their sheet, which received the lowest, and why.

• This is a list of characteristics for leaders, but every Christian should strive to have their life align with this list.
• Some issues are specifically for those inside the church to know and others are for those outside the church. We should be the same wherever we are.

• A leader in a church should have a good reputation among those who are a part of that church.

• *Temperate* is a broader concept that includes more than just alcohol (since Paul mentions that specifically in verse 3). It means being able to live with the tension that exists in this life. Moderation without excess in either direction is what we call balance.

• "Able to teach"—that is, more is caught than taught. It means being with your students all the time, not just for an hour each week. This way students could see whether or not their teacher lives what she talks about.

• "The husband of but one wife"—How does your church interpret this verse? Some say it means an elder has to be married. Some say that an elder must be married to one woman at a time. Some say that elders must stop being elders if their wives leave them—even if they die. Could a leader be divorced and still serve your church?

• Could a woman serve in a primary leadership role in your church?

"Not given to drunkenness, not violent but gentle, not quarrelsome, not a lover of money" (1 Timothy 3:3).

• Aristotle used the word that we use for *drunkenness* to convey the idea of being tipsy or having a buzz. It doesn't say "don't drink," but by using this word, it's implied that they shouldn't drink much.

• Drunkenness often leads to violence, quarrels, and accidents.

• The desire for money is one of the greatest traps used to capture Christian leaders. It was true then, and it's true now.

"He must manage his own family well and see that his children obey him with proper respect. (If anyone does not know how to manage his own family, how can he take care of God's church?)" (1 Timothy 3:4-5)

• Manage means the idea of a benevolent director, not a demanding dictator (Ephesians 5:28-6:9).

• Children can respect their parents because of their position or because of their performance. Parents would prefer that their children respect them because they know they are loved, and they want to express their love in return.

• Why would being a good parent make someone a good church leader?

"He must not be a recent convert, or he may become conceited and fall under the same judgment as the devil. He must also have a good reputation with outsiders, so that he will not fall into disgrace and into the devil's trap" (1 Timothy 3:6-7).

• Maturity is required of leaders. They should not only be spiritually mature, but also socially and emotionally mature, as well as mature in other areas. Not perfection—just progression.

• Maturity doesn't equal age, but it often comes with age.

• Maturity is not instant, and sometimes people are immature for too long.

• Satan was judged guilty of pride. Pride is the core sin that influences all other sins.

"Deacons, likewise, are to be men worthy of respect, sincere, not indulging in much wine, and not pursuing dishonest gain" (1 Timothy 3:8).

• *Deacon* means "one who serves" or "servant."

• The traditional view sees the men in Acts 6:1-6 as being the first group of Deacons.

• We consider terms like *deacon* or *elder* to be titles. However, in his original letter Paul probably described a role or responsibility in the church rather than creating a new leadership position or church office for people to fill.

"They must keep hold of the deep truths of the faith with a clear conscience. They must first be tested; and then if there is nothing against them, let them serve as deacons" (1 Timothy 3:9-10).

• Leadership is not based upon the amount of time volunteered, the amount of money donated, or a good family name. Leadership in the church should be built upon the fact that the person holds to the deep truths of the faith. People are not given responsibility without proving themselves worthy of the task. Grace is free; trust should be earned.

"In the same way, their wives are to be women worthy of respect, not malicious talkers but temperate and trustworthy in everything" (1 Timothy 3:11).

• Wives or deaconesses? The Greek word *gune* is used for both "woman" and "wife," so three things are possible:
1. This passage is only referring to the deacons' wives. However, the extra Greek word that would normally indicate that this is the meaning is not present.
2. It's referring to all women.
3. It simply means deaconesses or female deacons such as Phoebe in Romans 16:1.

"A deacon must be the husband of but one wife and must manage his children and his household well" (1 Timothy 3:12).

• How does this compare to the previous verses about elders and their families? Why do you think the two positions are so similar?

"Those who have served well gain an excellent standing and great assurance in their faith in Christ Jesus" (1 Timothy 3:13).

• Our assurance rests on what God has done for us, but it makes it easier to have assurance if your faith is being lived out and expressed in natural, God-honoring ways.

"Although I hope to come to you soon, I am writing you these instructions so that, if I am delayed, you will know how people ought to conduct themselves in God's household, which is the church of the living God, the pillar and foundation of the truth" (1 Timothy 3:14-15).

• In verses 14 and 15, Paul—an ideal leader—explains why this letter was written to them.

"Beyond all question, the mystery of godliness is great: He appeared in a body, was vindicated by the Spirit, was seen by angels, was preached among the nations, was believed on in the world, was taken up in glory" (1 Timothy 3:16).

• Then as Paul reflects upon the mystery of godliness and the wonder of the incarnation, he responds with an outburst of praise.

LIVE IT IN YOUR WORLD

OPTIONAL ACTIVITY
TELL US ABOUT YOURSELF

Ahead of time ask a student to write a list of questions to ask a leader in your church. They should prepare enough questions to make this a 10-to-15-minute interview in front of the whole group. Then arrange to have a church leader come to your meeting for the interview.

Some suggested questions—
• How long have you been a leader in our church?
• What are the most important character qualities to look for in a leader?
• How can teens help the church?
• What can teens do to be leaders today?

PUT IT IN YOUR HEART

"He must also have a good reputation with outsiders, so that he will not fall into disgrace and into the devil's trap" (1 Timothy 3:7).

SMALL GROUP QUESTIONS

1. Define leadership in your own words.
2. Would you ever want to lead a church as an adult?
3. Which of the leadership traits that Paul mentioned in this chapter do you struggle the most to imitate?
4. Which of the leadership traits that Paul mentioned in this chapter is easiest for you to imitate?
5. How does the kind of leadership that Paul talks about differ from the kind of leadership that's typically talked about in school, business, or the rest of life?
6. Who is your favorite leader of all time? What is it about him that attracts you to him?
7. Which leader in the church do you admire the most? Explain why you chose her.
8. How can you become a better leader?
9. Is everyone supposed to be a leader? Or is everyone supposed to pursue the character qualities of a leader?
10. Why does the idea of being a servant-leader make sense?
11. Describe a scene from a movie that portrays true leadership to you.
12. If you are not going to be a leader, what can you do to help a leader be successful?

CLOSING PRAYER

TRUSTWORTHY LEADERSHIP SAYINGS

Paul quoted an understood axiom for leadership when he said, "Here is a trustworthy saying: If anyone sets his heart on being an overseer, he desires a noble task" (1 Timothy 1:1). Look at the following contemporary quotes on leadership and circle the four that you believe to be the most *trustworthy*.

"Do not follow where the path may lead. Go instead where there is no path and leave a trail."
—*Unknown*

"An army of sheep led by a lion would defeat an army of lions led by a sheep."
—*Arab Proverb*

"Leadership: the art of getting someone else to do something you want done because he wants to do it."
—*Dwight D. Eisenhower*

"Leaders must be close enough to relate to others but far enough ahead to motivate them."
—*John Maxwell*

"Don't tell people how to do things. Tell them what to do and let them surprise you with their results."
—*General George Patton*

"If you wish to serve by leading, then you must lead by serving."
 —*Haddon Robinson*

"No one need aspire to leadership and the work of God who is not prepared to pay a price greater than his contemporaries and colleagues are willing to pay. True leadership always exacts a heavy toll on the whole man, and the more effective the leadership is, the higher the price to be paid."
—*J. Oswald Sanders*

"No one deserves the right to lead without first persevering through pain and heartache and failure."
—*Charles Swindoll*

"If you wish to be a leader, you will be frustrated, for very few people wish to be led. If you aim to be a servant, you will never be frustrated."
—*Frank P. Warren*

"Management is doing things right; leadership is doing the right things."
 —*Peter Drucker and Warren Bennis*

WHAT DO YOU LOOK FOR IN A LEADER?

1. List the three greatest leaders of the past 100 years.

_____

_____

_____

2. Now list three things about each leader (in your list above) that made him great.

_____

_____

_____

3. List the three greatest leaders of all time.

_____

_____

_____

4. Now list three things about each leader (from your list in question three) that made her great.

_____

_____

_____

"The Lord does not look at the things man looks at. Man looks at the outward appearance, but the Lord looks at the heart" (1 Samuel 16:7).

COMPARE AND CONTRAST

Have you ever seen one of those puzzles containing two seemingly identical cartoon pictures where you have to find the six or seven little things that are different between the two? In the same way Paul's two lists of leadership guidelines found in 1 Timothy and Titus were not identical to each other, but they were very similar.

List the church leadership characteristics you find in each passage. Then put a star or some other symbol next to the ones that are the same in both lists. Notice the remaining church leadership characteristics that are different between the lists.

Titus 1:6-9   1 Timothy 3:2-9

1. _____   1. _____

2. _____   2. _____

3. _____   3. _____

4. _____   4. _____

5. _____   5. _____

6. _____   6. _____

7. _____   7. _____

8. _____   8. _____

9. _____   9. _____

10. _____   10. _____

BIBLICAL LEADERSHIP TRAITS

For each leadership quality below, circle the number that represents how important it is to you that a leader possesses that particular trait (0 = "It doesn't bother me if a leader isn't this way"; 5 = "I don't care one way or another"; 10 = "If I'm going to listen to them, then they'd better have this quality!").

1. Be above reproach
   1   2   3   4   5   6   7   8   9   10

2. The husband of but one wife
   1   2   3   4   5   6   7   8   9   10

3. Temperate
   1   2   3   4   5   6   7   8   9   10

4. Self-controlled
   1   2   3   4   5   6   7   8   9   10

5. Respectable
   1   2   3   4   5   6   7   8   9   10

6. Hospitable
   1   2   3   4   5   6   7   8   9   10

7. Able to teach
   1   2   3   4   5   6   7   8   9   10

8. Not given to drunkenness
   1   2   3   4   5   6   7   8   9   10

9. Not violent but gentle
   1   2   3   4   5   6   7   8   9   10

10. Not quarrelsome
    1   2   3   4   5   6   7   8   9   10

11. Not a lover of money
    1   2   3   4   5   6   7   8   9   10

12. Manages his own family well
    1   2   3   4   5   6   7   8   9   10

13. He must not be a recent convert
    1   2   3   4   5   6   7   8   9   10

14. He must also have a good reputation with outsiders
    1   2   3   4   5   6   7   8   9   10

15. Holy and disciplined
    1   2   3   4   5   6   7   8   9   10

16. He must hold firmly to the trustworthy message as it has been taught
    1   2   3   4   5   6   7   8   9   10

From Creative Bible Lessons in 1 & 2 Timothy and Titus by Len Evans. Permission to reproduce this page granted only for use in buyer's own youth group. ©2004 by Youth Specialties. www.YouthSpecialties.com

get in shape!

TRAINING TO BE GODLY

session 5

During this session students will—

- Discuss different spiritual habits they can adopt as they train to be godly.
- Be exposed to many types of lifestyle spirituality.
- Be challenged to incorporate some new spiritual habits into their lifestyle.

THE BIG IDEA

Students can train themselves to be godly. This lesson will be short on instruction and long on application.

BACKGROUND CHECK

Training to be godly is not an occasional event but rather an ongoing attitude that is accompanied by actions. An old saying goes, "The journey of a thousand miles starts with the first step." Consider this to be the first step of training yourself to be godly because our faith is a lifelong journey.

OPENING

Option 1: You've Got Potential!

Share the following examples with your students. Say something like—

Training is a word that is often associated with athletes. And some world-class athletes have renowned workout regimens. Let's compare the records of two basketball players.

First, Larry "The Legend" Bird. In 13 seasons he was a 12-time NBA All-Star, three-time MVP, three-time Long Distance Shootout Winner; won three championships; and was declared one of the 50 greatest basketball players of all time. He had great skills, but his workout routine was legendary in itself. He regularly showed up at practice sessions two hours ahead of everybody else. There, alone on the court, he would shoot hundreds of set shots and free throws every day.

And then there is Earl "The Goat" Manigault. Have you heard of him? Earl was a New York City playground legend who has been called the greatest basketball player the world has never known. He could leap and pick a quarter off of the top of the backboard despite being just a little over six feet tall. In a New York Times article, Kareem Abdul-Jabbar once said Manigault was "the best basketball player of his size in the history of New York City." But Earl became addicted to heroin, and by the time he got himself cleaned up and was given a tryout to play professional basketball, his skills were gone at the age of 25.

Both men had potential from a young age, but only one was able to make the most of his potential. Training and discipline helped make Larry Bird a great player; bad decisions and a lack of discipline ruined Earl Manigault's life. In 1998 he died at the age of 55. Regrets are made of potential not realized.

If you are to reach for your spiritual potential, you must have a plan in place to train yourself to be godly—and you must do it. Often when we do a Bible study lesson like this, we have to wrestle with how to put it into action in our lives, or we struggle to discover what a verse means. Our primary text in this session is very straightforward, so we will spend a lot of time discovering different ways to put this Scripture into action.

Option 2: Extreme Sports

Start by saying something like—

Over the last 10 years the world has embraced extreme sports through competitions like the X-games. Everyone seems to want to push the limit—or at least watch others push the limits. People who are extreme stand out and get noticed!

Divide your students into groups of three or four and ask them to come up with two *extreme* people who get a lot of attention because they are not normal or because they surpass their peers in their profession or approach to life. (For example, Billy Graham is an extreme Christian. He is in his 80s and has talked to over 210 million people in over 185 countries or territories about Jesus. Billy is extreme!)

After a few minutes ask the groups to share the names of one or two extreme people and why they chose them.

Then say something like—

How much time should we invest to train ourselves in biblical truth? How are we training ourselves in godliness? We should not have regrets about not studying God's truth. Regrets are made up of potential not realized.

If you are to reach for your spiritual potential, you must have a plan in place to train yourself to be godly—and you must do it. Often when we do a Bible study lesson like this, we have to wrestle with how to put it into action in our lives or we struggle to discover what a verse means. Our primary text in this session is very straightforward, so we will spend a lot of time discovering different ways to put this Scripture into action.

READ IT IN GOD'S WORD
"Have nothing to do with godless myths and old wives' tales" (1 Timothy 4:7).

• Timothy was brought up in the faith by his mother and grandmother. By knowing God's word, he was able to discern between truths and myths. The false teachers taught some truth, but not everything they said was true. He was to have nothing to do with false teaching in the church.

ACTIVITY
TRUE OR FALSE (TEACHING) QUIZ

You'll need—
• Copies of **True or False (Teaching) Quiz** (page 57) for each student
• Pen or pencil for each student

Say something like—

Sometimes it's easy to distinguish between biblical truths, and sometimes it isn't. Let's see how you do with a short quiz.

Hand out the quiz sheets and something to write with, then give the students time to work on it individually. After they complete the quiz, review the answers with them (false, false, true, false, false, true [Mark 5:3], false, and false). Transition back into the lesson with something like—

No matter what your score, we can all improve in the area of our spiritual strength. That's what Paul talks about next.

"Rather, train yourself to be godly" (1 Timothy 4:7).

• Paul uses athletic imagery in his writings (1 Corinthians 9:24-27; Galatians 5:7; 2 Timothy 4:7) to show spiritual truths. The Greek word that Paul uses for train is where we get our words for gymnastics and gymnasium.

"For physical training is of some value" (1 Timothy 4:8).

• This is good.

"But godliness has value for all things, holding promise for both the present life and the life to come" (1 Timothy 4:8).

• This is better!
• When we train to become godly, there is a benefit in our current life (before death) and our future life (after death).
• The present benefits—We become more and more like Christ in our life and our love toward God and others.

• The future benefits—God will reward us for our faithful service, and we hope to hear Jesus say, "Well done, good and faithful servant."

"This is a trustworthy saying that deserves full acceptance" (1 Timothy 4:9).

• Paul used the phrase "trustworthy saying" only five times in all of his writings—and all instances are found in 1 Timothy, 2 Timothy, and Titus!

"(And for this we labor and strive), that we have put our hope in the living God, who is the Savior of all men, and especially of those who believe" (1 Timothy 4:10).

• In order to understand what Paul means when he writes "Savior of all men," we need to look back in 1 Timothy at the two previous times he used the phrase "all men." They are found in 1 Timothy 2:3-6: "This is good, and pleases God our Savior, who wants all men to be saved and to come to a knowledge of the truth. For there is one God and one mediator between God and men, the man Christ Jesus, who gave himself as a ransom for all men—the testimony given in its proper time."

LIVE IT IN YOUR WORLD

ACTIVITY
PRAY AS THE SPIRIT LEADS

You'll need—
• A tea candle for each student
• More pillar candles stationed around the room, including a *center candle* up front
• Matches or a lighter
• Paper and pencils for students who wish to do prayer journaling during this time
• Bible verses from **Pray as the Spirit Leads** (pages 58-59) copied and cut apart into strips

Allow at least 15 to 20 minutes for this activity. Using this idea with your group will be a stretch of your faith because you have no control over what will happen once it gets going. Before you do it try to cover this time in prayer for a week. You may wish to use this as a closing for your lesson, or you could also expand it into a normal worship service with your kids.

If you can, create atmosphere in the room by having some lit candles and by having a tea candle for every student. When you are ready, transition with something like—

This is when I would typically give a message that involves God's Word. Today we are going to do something a little different. We are just going to read different sections of the Scripture out loud and listen for God to speak to us.

Psalm 119:18 says, "Open my eyes that I may see wonderful things in your law." We know the Holy Spirit is given to believers, and part of his ministry is to reveal God's truth to us. So that's what we are going to do. We are going to take God at his word, about his Word, and expect him to speak directly to us.

I'm going to hand out slips of paper with Bible verses written on them. After the verses are read, or even after a single verse has been read, you are invited to respond to whatever God is saying to you by praying out loud, by writing down your prayer to God, or by doing whatever you feel led to do.

We're going to have silence—starting now—and you are invited to pray individually. I encourage you to pray for your own spiritual life and for your neighbor. After you have prayed, come light your candle from the center candle and leave it here on the table as a sign that you are ready to hear from God. We'll begin reading the Scriptures when all the candles are lit.

After the time of silence and when you are ready to begin the reading, pray something along these lines—

Father,
Thank you for what you have done already today and thank you for what you are going to do as we hear your voice through the Scriptures you have given to us. Open our eyes so that we may see the wonderful things in your Word and open our hearts to do wonderful things in your world. In the name of Jesus, the Living Word, we pray. Amen.

IDEAS
THERE ARE DIFFERENT WAYS YOU CAN DO THE READINGS:

- Out loud in unison
- Responsive reading style
- Individuals from different locations in the room alternate reading the verses
- Read different translations of the same passage

If you plan to end your meeting with this activity, after all the verses have been read and people are finished praying, extinguish the candles to let the kids know they are dismissed.

(Note: For more details about these and other spiritual practices, pick up Soul Shaper: Exploring Spirituality and Contemplative Practices in Youth Ministry *by Tony Jones.)*

PUT IT IN YOUR HEART
"Have nothing to do with godless myths and old wives' tales; rather, train yourself to be godly. For physical training is of some value, but godliness has value for all things, holding promise for both the present life and the life to come" (1 Timothy 4:7-8).

SMALL GROUP QUESTIONS
1. What did you believe as a child that you no longer believe?
2. What are the earthly benefits of being godly in this life?
3. What grade would you give yourself regarding your current training in godliness?
4. What would you like your grade to be? How are you going to get there? (Pass out copies of **The 21-Day Quiet Time Challenge**, p. 60, to the group and encourage them to do it.)
5. Which of the spiritual practices that we covered appeal to you?
6. Is God the Savior of all men?
7. Are all men saved?
8. How do the three times that Paul uses the phrase "all men" relate to each other?
9. How can we better understand 1 Timothy 4:10 by knowing 1 Timothy 2:3-6? Explain your answers.
10. Which of Brad Cecil's ideas of spiritual formation appeals to you? Why? What path of spiritual formation would you add?

CLOSING PRAYER

TRUE OR FALSE (TEACHING) QUIZ

_____ 1. The Holy Spirit is similar to "the force" in *Star Wars*.

_____ 2. Jesus always existed, but he became the Son of God when he became human.

_____ 3. Jesus believed and taught that Satan was a real angelic being, not just a symbol of evil.

_____ 4. Jesus was the archangel Michael before he became human.

_____ 5. Jesus went to North America after the resurrection and ascension to speak to Native Americans.

_____ 6. Jesus had sisters and brothers.

_____ 7. Jesus said, "I am the River of Life."

_____ 8. Jesus was a prophet for God.

PRAY AS THE SPIRIT LEADS

"Devote yourself to the public reading of Scripture" (1 Timothy 4:13).

"Hear, O Israel: The Lord our God, the Lord is one. Love the Lord your God with all your heart and with all your soul and with all your strength. These commandments that I give you today are to be upon your hearts" (Deuteronomy 6: 4-6, NIV).

"He humbled you, causing you to hunger and then feeding you with manna, which neither you nor your fathers had known, to teach you that man does not live on bread alone but on every word that comes from the mouth of the Lord" (Deuteronomy 8:3, NIV).

"Be strong and courageous. Do not be afraid or terrified because of them, for the Lord your God goes with you; he will never leave you nor forsake you" (Deuteronomy 31:6, NIV).

"But the LORD said to Samuel, 'Do not consider his appearance or his height, for I have rejected him. The LORD does not look at the things man looks at. Man looks at the outward appearance, but the LORD looks at the heart'" (1 Samuel 16:7, NIV).

"So on October 8 Ezra the priest brought the scroll of the law before the assembly, which included the men and women and all the children old enough to understand. He faced the square just inside the Water Gate from early morning until noon and read aloud to everyone who could understand. All the people paid close attention to the Book of the Law" (Nehemiah 8:2-3, NLT).

"Ezra praised the great LORD God, and the people shouted, 'Amen! Amen!' Then they bowed with their faces to the ground and worshiped the LORD" (Nehemiah 8:6, CEV).

"Blessed is the man who does not walk in the counsel of the wicked or stand in the way of sinners or sit in the seat of mockers. But his delight is in the law of the LORD, and on his law he meditates day and night. He is like a tree planted by streams of water, which yields its fruit in season and whose leaf does not wither. Whatever he does prospers" (Psalm 1:1-3, NIV).

"O Lord, our Lord, how majestic is your name in all the earth! You have set your glory above the heavens. From the lips of children and infants you have ordained praise because of your enemies, to silence the foe and the avenger. When I consider your heavens, the work of your fingers, the moon and the stars, which you have set in place, what is man that you are mindful of him, the son of man that you care for him?" (Psalm 8:1-4, NIV).

From Creative Bible Lessons in 1 & 2 Timothy and Titus by Len Evans. Permission to reproduce this page granted only for use in buyer's own youth group. ©2004 by Youth Specialties. www.YouthSpecialties.com

"When I kept silent, my bones wasted away through my groaning all day long. For day and night your hand was heavy upon me; my strength was sapped as in the heat of summer" (Psalm 32:3-4, NIV).

"For troubles without number surround me; my sins have overtaken me, and I cannot see. They are more than the hairs of my head, and my heart fails within me. Be pleased, O Lord, to save me; O Lord, come quickly to help me" (Psalm 40:12-13, NIV).

"Be still, and know that I am God; I will be exalted among the nations, I will be exalted in the earth" (Psalm 46:10, NIV).

"Cast your cares on the Lord and he will sustain you; he will never let the righteous fall" (Psalm 55:22, NIV).

"For as high as the heavens are above the earth, so great is his love for those who fear him; as far as the east is from the west, so far has he removed our transgressions from us. As a father has compassion on his children, so the Lord has compassion on those who fear him" (Psalm 103:11-13, NIV).

"Search me, O God, and know my heart; test me and know my anxious thoughts. See if there is any offensive way in me, and lead me in the way everlasting" (Psalm 139:23-24, NIV).

"Trust in the Lord with all your heart and lean not on your own understanding; in all your ways acknowledge him, and he will make your paths straight" (Proverbs 3:5-6, NIV).

"For even the Son of Man did not come to be served, but to serve, and to give his life as a ransom for many" (Mark 10:45, NIV).

"For God so loved the world that he gave his one and only Son, that whoever believes in him shall not perish but have eternal life. For God did not send his Son into the world to condemn the world, but to save the world through him. Whoever believes in him is not condemned, but whoever does not believe stands condemned already because he has not believed in the name of God's one and only Son" (John 3:16-18, NIV).

THE 21-DAY QUIET TIME CHALLENGE

Spend 10 minutes a day (about one percent of your 16 waking hours) in God's Word for the next three weeks. This consistent time spent in Scripture, prayer, and reflection can rekindle your love for God and his Word. As you read the daily passage, keep these points in mind—

1. Pray. Ask the Holy Spirit to guide you into all truth.
2. Look. What did this passage mean to those who heard it? What's the main point?
3. Reflect. What's God saying to me through these words?
4. Live. How should my life change because of these truths? Should I start doing something, or should I stop doing something? What am I going to feel, think, and believe because of this passage?

Day 1—Genesis 1: Creation

Day 2—Luke 2: Jesus' Birth

Day 3—Genesis 3: Why Jesus Was Born (first Messianic prophecy, 3:15)

Day 4—Psalm 51: A Prayer of Confession

Day 5—Matthew 5: The Sermon on the Mount (Read chapters 6–7, too, for AP credit.)

Day 6—Genesis 12: God Chooses Abraham

Day 7—Hebrews 11: The Christian Hall of Fame

Day 8—Exodus 3: God Chooses Moses

Day 9—John 17: Jesus' Prayer for His Disciples

Day 10—Exodus 20: God's Gift of the Law

Day 11—Romans 3: God's Gift of Grace

Day 12—Luke 24: The Resurrection

Day 13—Psalm 23: The Lord Is My Shepherd

Day 14—Romans 12: Be Transformed

Day 15—1 Samuel 17: David and Goliath

Day 16—1 Timothy 4: Leadership Instructions

Day 17—Isaiah 53: The Suffering Servant

Day 18—1 Peter 2: Spiritual Growth Prepares You for Suffering

Day 19—Daniel 6: Daniel in the Lion's Den

Day 20—Ephesians 6: Spiritual Warfare

Day 21—Revelation 22: We Win in the End

living your faith on monday and beyond

EXTRAORDINARY FAITH IN THE ORDINARY WORLD

session 6

During this session students will—

- Realize that while people may not respect them initially because of their young age, people might respect them eventually because of who they are.
- Understand that continued spiritual maturity requires a plan to grow within a community of believers.
- Be encouraged to view their faith in a holistic manner and not categorize different areas of their lives.

■ THE BIG IDEA

Age does not determine spiritual maturity or spiritual growth, but attitude and actions do.

■ BACKGROUND CHECK

Read all of 1 Timothy 4 to learn the context of our next passage of Scripture. Remind your students of the interwoven theme throughout the Pastoral Epistles.

DID YOU KNOW?

HOW YOUNG IS *YOUNG*?

In the culture when this letter was written, the word for young meant anyone under the age of 40 who was able to serve in the military. Timothy was not a teenage pastor. However, he may have been as young as 17 when he met Paul and joined him on his first missionary journey. Imagine putting "internship with the apostle Paul" on your college application! He was probably in his early to mid-30s when he received this letter.

Chapter 4 includes specific instructions to Timothy, the pastor/leader of the Church of Ephesus. Most of us will not become pastors of a church, but we can still learn from the instructions Paul gave to Timothy. In order to do this we must first discover what Paul told him and then discern how we adapt and apply the truths in our world today. The message in chapter 4 is at the heart of any biblical pastoral ministry. Since every believer is to be active in ministry (Ephesians 4:11-15), we can learn from Paul's instructions how we can also become better ministers. We must watch and grow in two basic areas—our own lives (1 Timothy 4:11-12) and our own beliefs (1 Timothy 4:13-16).

God has given us his Word (vs. 13) and spiritual gifts (vs. 14), and we must give ourselves back to God (vv. 15-16) for the benefit of others.

OPENING
Option 1: Movie Clip
Matilda

You'll need—
- *Matilda* (Columbia TriStar, 1996)
- TV and DVD player

Share a story from your own life about a time when it was difficult being young. Maybe you felt misunderstood by your parents, a teacher, or someone else who was older than you; maybe someone picked on you.

Now play the clip from *Matilda*, a story about a girl who was born to uncaring and insensitive parents. In this scene Matilda is belittled and humiliated by her father.

Start 00:21:55 Harry Wormwood (Danny DeVito) is standing in a used car lot, and he says, "Michael, one day all this will be yours."

Stop 00:23:45 Harry says, "I'm smart; you're dumb! I'm big; you're little! I'm right; you're wrong! And there's nothing you can do about it!"

After the clip ends, ask—

- *Why do parents sometimes talk down to their kids?*
- *Do you think most adults look down on students? What's happened to you to make you think that way?*
- *How do you handle it when others look down on you?*

Encourage their participation and transition into the lesson with something like—

Sometimes no matter what we do, others will look down on us. When we act immaturely, it's understandable if adults don't think the best of us; but when we are maturing, we are also showing them that we deserve their respect. Timothy had a similar problem. Let's look at what Paul told him.

Option 2: Phobophobiac Quiz

You'll need—
- Copies of the **Phobophobiac Quiz** (page 67) for each student
- Pen or pencil for each student

As students enter the room, distribute the **Phobophobiac Quiz** (page 67). Students can work on this quiz either individually or in groups of four or less. Tell them not to start working on it until after you have given them the instructions. After a few minutes, go over the following answers with them:

Coulrophobia = fear of clowns
Ecclesiophobia = fear of church
Ephebiphobia = fear of teenagers
Gerascophobia = fear of growing old
Hippopotomonstrosesquippedaliophobia = fear of long words

Homilophobia = fear of sermons
Hypengyophobia = fear of responsibility
Peladophobia = fear of bald people
Phobophobia = fear of phobias
Scolionophobia = fear of school
Staurophobia = fear of crosses
Triskaidekaphobia = fear of the number 13
Uranophobia = fear of Heaven
Xenoglossophobia = fear of foreign languages

Then say—

When we are immature, it's understandable if adults don't think the best of us; but when we are maturing, we are also showing them that we deserve their respect. Timothy had a similar problem. Let's look at what Paul told him.

READ IT IN GOD'S WORD
Read 1 Timothy 4:11-16 to the students.

You'll need—
• Bibles
• A copy of **Say What?** (page 68) for each student
• Pen or pencil for each student

Pass out **Say What?** (page 68) and lead students through it. After they've completed their personalized version of 1 Timothy 4:11-16, jump into the text again by explaining some things to them—

The passage we're studying was written expressly to one person, Timothy. So what good does it do the rest of us? There are three helpful steps you can take to transfer the biblical truths of yesterday into the reality of today and tomorrow—

> • *First step: Discover the specific prescription Paul gave to Timothy by asking, "What did Paul say?"*
> • *Second step: Decide what it meant to Timothy by asking, "What did it mean to Timothy?"*
> • *Third step. Discern what it means to you by asking, "How can I put these truths into action?"*

"Command and teach these things" (1 Timothy 4:11).

• *Command* and *teach* are related words with different meanings. Command deals with the role of confrontation (mainly with the false teachers and false teaching that were mentioned earlier in the book). Teach deals with the role of instructing the believers.
• "These things" refers to the entire book in general but specifically the section that follows.

"Don't let anyone look down on you because you are young, but set an example for the believers in speech, in life, in love, in faith and in purity" (1 Timothy 4:12).

• Timothy was in his early to mid-30s, but the principle is that anyone can become a model of maturity (we are told how to become a model in verse 16). People might not respect you initially because of how old you are, but you can eventually earn their respect because of who you are.
• As you examine your behavior, a good question to consider is, "If you were being prosecuted for being a Christian, would there be enough evidence?"

• Love is the central component that impacts your public life and your private life. If you are failing in your speech, your life, your faith, or your purity, then you are failing in your love!
• Unless your private faith is authentic and growing, you won't be able to maintain a facade of strong faith for too long.

"Until I come, devote yourself to the public reading of Scripture, to preaching and to teaching" (1 Timothy 4:13).

• Preaching is better translated as *exhortation*, which includes explaining and applying the passages that were read.

"Do not neglect your gift, which was given you through a prophetic message when the body of elders laid their hands on you" (1 Timothy 4:14).

• "Timothy's image of himself as a minister was evidently deficient…If others were not to look down on Timothy, neither was he to look down on himself" (from the *Bible Knowledge Commentary*).
• Every believer has the gift of the Spirit and at least one gift from the Spirit.

"Be diligent in these matters; give yourself wholly to them, so that everyone may see your progress" (1 Timothy 4:15).

• "Be diligent" or "give careful thought to." You need to have a plan or a process in place if you are to make progress.
• The phrase "wholly to them" gives the impression of being totally consumed by them. In other words, our faith is a 24/7 commitment.
• Everyone (not just believers) will see Timothy's progress, and this will take care of the problem of people looking down on him.
• God's concern is not for you to earn the good reputation of "Mr. or Miss Holiness of the Universe" but for you to be salt and light to the world so that others may hear more about his great reputation—as a holy, merciful, loving, gracious, and forgiving God—and believe in him, too.

"Watch your life and doctrine closely. Persevere in them, because if you do, you will save both yourself and your hearers" (1 Timothy 4:16).

• You believe and then receive salvation as a free gift, but you progress in your salvation as God keeps working in you, bringing about continual changes (see Philippians 2:12-13).
• Faith in action is an attraction. God wants to and will use you to reach your friends. When you watch yourself and your beliefs—and when your behavior matches your beliefs—God will use you to strengthen your Christian friends and reach your non-Christian friends for him.

LIVE IT IN YOUR WORLD

You'll need—
• Bibles
• Pen or pencil for each student
• A copy of **Watch Your Life and Doctrine** (pages 69-70) for each student
• A copy of **How's Your Progress?** (page 71) for each student

The **Watch Your Life and Doctrine** handout (pages 69-70) helps students evaluate where they are in their spiritual walk; the **How's Your Progress?** handout (page 71) helps students evaluate how they will change. Divide into smaller groups of students, preferably with an adult leader in each to facilitate discussion, and have the groups go through the two pages together.

PUT IT IN YOUR HEART

"Don't let anyone look down on you because you are young, but set an example for the believers in speech, in life, in love, in faith and in purity" (1 Timothy 4:12).

SMALL GROUP QUESTIONS

1. If you were on trial for being a Christian, would there be enough evidence to convict you of being a believer?
2. Are you in any relationship right now in which you need to confront someone over something they've done or said? How are you going to talk to them?
3. What gifts has God given you? Are you using them?
4. How have others encouraged you to serve?
5. What are some negative ways we use our speech (gossip, slander, lying, making fun of someone, etc.)? Which of these is the hardest one for you to deal with?
6. What are some positive ways we use our speech (encouraging others, remaining silent when you want to talk, promoting others instead of tearing them down)?
7. What's harder to keep pure—your mind, your heart, or your body?
8. What things pollute our minds?
9. What things pollute our hearts?
10. What things pollute our bodies?
11. If God could give you any character trait as a gift, which one would you want?
12. What will you do this next week to watch your life and doctrine closely?

CLOSING PRAYER

PHOBOPHOBIAC QUIZ

Draw a line to match the name of the phobia with the fear.

Fear of clowns	Homilophobia
Fear of church	Hippopotomonstrosesquippedaliophobia
Fear of teenagers	Staurophobia
Fear of growing old	Gerascophobia
Fear of sermons	Ecclesiophobia
Fear of responsibility	Hypengyophobia
Fear of phobias	Coulrophobia
Fear of the number 13	Uranophobia
Fear of long words	Peladophobia
Fear of crosses	Ephebiphobia
Fear of foreign languages	Xenoglossophobia
Fear of school	Triskaidekaphobia
Fear of bald people	Scolionophobia
Fear of Heaven	Phobophobia

Found on The Phobia List Web site (http://www.phobialist.com)

SAY WHAT?

Sometimes the Bible is difficult to understand because we have to overcome so many obstacles to know what the author originally meant. We have to overcome a language hurdle, a time hurdle, location hurdle, a cultural hurdle, and more. Some people have paraphrased the Bible to make it easier to understand. What's the difference between a paraphrase of the Bible and a translation of the Bible?

Read both of the following versions of 1 Timothy 4:11-16.

"Stress these things and teach them. Don't let anybody look down his nose at you just because you're a young man. Instead, you be an example of what church members should be in speech, in conduct, in love, in faith, in dedication. Till I come, keep up your reading, your counseling, your teaching. Care for the inner spiritual gift which was prophetically bestowed on you when the elders laid their hands on you. Let these things consume you; breathe them, so that it will be clear to everybody that you're making progress. Keep a tight check on yourself and your teaching. Stay on the ball, for by doing so you will save both yourself and those that listen to you" (1 Timothy 4:11-16, The Cotton Patch Version).

"Teach these things and insist that everyone learn them. Don't let anyone think less of you because you are young. Be an example to all believers in what you teach, in the way you live, in your love, your faith, and your purity. Until I get there, focus on reading the Scriptures to the church, encouraging the believers, and teaching them. Do not neglect the spiritual gift you received through the prophecies spoken to you when the elders of the church laid their hands on you. Give your complete attention to these matters. Throw yourself into your tasks so that everyone will see your progress. Keep a close watch on yourself and on your teaching. Stay true to what is right, and God will save you and those who hear you" (1 Timothy 4:11-16, The New Living Translation).

Which version did you like best?

Now create your own version of 1 Timothy 4:11-16.

The _____ Version
          (insert your name here)

_____

_____

_____

_____

_____

_____

_____

_____

WATCH YOUR LIFE AND DOCTRINE

	Don't Watch Your Life	Do Watch Your Life
Don't Watch Your Doctrine	**I.** **REBEL**	**II.** **PHARISEE**
Do Watch Your Doctrine	**III.** **HYPOCRITE**	**IV.** **GROWING DISCIPLE**

I. If you don't watch your life or your doctrine closely, you are a rebel. This could be a Christian or a non-Christian. If you consider yourself to be a Christian and you are living this way, you need to reevaluate where your life is heading and make sure you really believe. And if you do really believe, then you need to change your behavior and repent.

II. If you watch your life closely but not your doctrine, you are a Pharisee. Pharisees were the religious leaders of Jesus' day. He had the harshest words for these guys.

III. If you watch your doctrine closely but not your life, you are a hypocrite. You might believe the truth but live a lie; you are a weak believer.

IV. If you watch your life and your doctrine closely, you are a growing disciple. This shows progress in godliness, not perfection. This doesn't mean there won't be valleys or "dark nights of the soul" in your life but that through even your hardest times you are able to rely upon God and his promises.

1. Should a Christian mess with a Ouija™ board?

2. Is it okay for a Christian to read horoscopes? Why or why not?

3. List different ways that we can train ourselves to be godly.

4. Which of these is the hardest for you to do? Why?

6. If something is really important to you, don't you make the time to do it (eating, exercise)? Then why do so few Christians make time to be with God?

7. How could Jesus be "the Savior of all Men" without saving everybody?

8. What are some negative ways we use our speech?

9. What are some positive ways we use our speech?

10. What's harder to keep pure—your mind, your heart, or your body?

11. What pollutes our minds? What pollutes our hearts? What pollutes our bodies?

12. If God could give you any character trait as a gift, what would you want?

13. What will you do this next week to watch your life and doctrine closely?

14. Salvation is a process—

    a. Belief in Christ (conversion)

    b. New life in the Spirit (regeneration)

    c. Becoming like Christ (sanctification—Philippians 2:12-13)

    d. Joining Christ for eternity (glorification). So is Paul saying that we can be saved by something besides grace?

HOW'S YOUR PROGRESS?

"You can't build a reputation on what you are going to do." —Henry Ford

You are already an example to your friends and family of what a Christian looks like. Are you a good example or a bad one? Decide how you will become a better example in the five areas Paul shares with Timothy.

"Sow a thought, reap an act.
Sow an act, reap a habit.
Sow a habit, reap a character.
Sow a character, reap a destiny."
—Anonymous

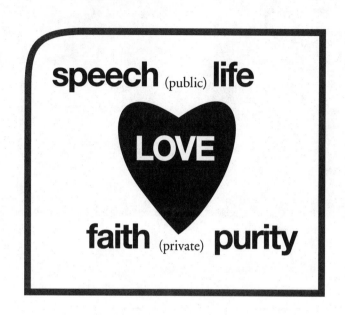

Speech
• How often do I encourage others?
• How often do I talk about others?
• When was the last time I didn't say the first thing that came to my mind?
• Is it easy for me to lie? How can I stop doing that?
• How do I speak the truth in love (Ephesians 4:15) when…
> • my friend has bad breath?
> • my friend is dating a non-Christian?
> • my friend is being a jerk to other people?

Life
• What can you do to put Romans 12:2 into action? Who can regularly help you do this?

Love
• Do I love my friends more now than I did six months ago?
• Am I praying for my friends and enemies like God commands?
• Good speech and a good life without love are worthless (1 Corinthians 13).

Faith
• Do you have a plan to grow in your faith?
Whether it's through prayer, Bible study, a small group, worship, journaling, serving, singing, solitude, fasting, or any other of the many spiritual habits, you need to know what works for you and work on improving it. These things are not the way to God, but they can enable you to be strengthened by God.

Purity
• How do you maintain purity in your speech, life, love, and faith?

People might not respect you initially because of how old you are, but you can eventually earn their respect because of who you are.

watch your enemy

AVOID SATAN'S TRAPS

session 7

During this session students will—

- Discover that pride is at the center of every sinner and the root of every sin.
- Learn that the same thing that trapped the devil can trap Christians, especially Christians who are young in their faith.

■ THE BIG IDEA

Our spiritual enemy is real even though the enemy cannot be seen. We know our enemy is real because of what God has revealed to us through different passages of Scripture.

QUOTE

"The greatest trick the devil ever pulled was convincing the world he didn't exist."
—Verbal Kint (*The Usual Suspects*)

■ BACKGROUND CHECK

Satan is referred to four times in the Pastoral Epistles:

"Among them are Hymenaeus and Alexander, whom I have handed over to Satan to be taught not to blaspheme" (1 Timothy 1:20).

"He must not be a recent convert, or he may become conceited and fall under the same judgment as the devil. He must also have a good reputation with outsiders, so that he will not fall into disgrace and into the devil's trap" (1 Timothy 3:6-7).

"So I counsel younger widows to marry, to have children, to manage their homes and to give the enemy no opportunity for slander. Some have in fact already turned away to follow Satan" (1 Timothy 5:14-15).

"And that they will come to their senses and escape from the trap of the devil, who has taken them captive to do his will" (2 Timothy 2:26).

We learned in chapter 1 that Timothy was the pastor at the church in Ephesus, so his church was the initial recipient of the letter Paul sent to the Ephesians. Furthermore, Ephesians 6 is probably the chapter in the Bible referred to the most when one teaches about spiritual warfare and Satan. Read Ephesians 6:10-18 and keep it in mind as you prepare and teach this lesson:

"Finally, be strong in the Lord and in his mighty power. Put on the full armor of God so that you can take your stand against the devil's schemes. For our struggle is not against flesh and blood, but against the rulers, against the authorities, against the powers of this dark world and against the spiritual forces of evil in the heavenly realms. Therefore put on the full armor of God, so that when the day of evil comes, you may be able to stand your ground, and after you have done everything, to stand. Stand firm then, with the belt of truth buckled around your waist, with the breastplate of righteousness in place, and with your feet fitted with the readiness that comes from the gospel of peace. In addition to all this, take up the shield of faith, with which you can extinguish all the flaming arrows of the evil one. Take the helmet of salvation and the sword of the Spirit, which is the word of God. And pray in the Spirit on all occasions with all kinds of prayers and requests. With this in mind, be alert and always keep on praying for all the saints."

OPENING

Option 1: Blindfolded Obstacle Relay

Before the meeting begins, set up tables, chairs, drums, the senior pastor—basically whatever is available—in a room. Form one to three teams based on the size of your group. Each team should have three students. The remaining students can either cheer or try to distract the participants at the appropriate times. Blindfold one participant from each team at a time. Have them walk about 90 feet, retrieve something, and then return. Only the blindfolded person goes through the obstacle course.

The first blindfolded student looks at the obstacles then puts the blindfold on and has to go through the course without any help. The second blindfolded student looks at the obstacles, but their teammates get to yell instructions while other students yell false instructions. The third student looks at the obstacles, puts the blindfold on, and then is instructed to take the blindfold off and go through the obstacle course. Time each team and give the results.

Transition with something like this—

That was obviously an unfair competition. We'd all rather be the person who gets to compete without a blindfold. Some people walk through life blind and alone, others are blinded with people yelling at them, and still others are able to see clearly. Satan wants to blind you to his strategies. Today we'll look at some truths about the devil who tries to deceive you so you will be aware of his schemes.

Option 2: Movie Clip
The Emperor's New Groove

You'll need—
• *The Emperor's New Groove* (Walt Disney, 2000)
• TV and DVD player

Start 00:26:15 Kuzco (the narrator) says, "Ugh, he's doing his own theme music?"

Stop 00:27:38 Kronk says, "That'll work."

Kronk (voice of Patrick Warburton) talks with his shoulder angel and his shoulder demon after throwing an unconscious Emperor Kuzco (voice of David Spade) into the water. Get them into the movie by asking a few questions like—

• *Have you ever felt like you had two different voices in your mind telling you what do?*
• *How do you know which voice to listen to?*

- *What were some of the false ideas about angels and demons portrayed in that scene?*
- *What were some of the truths about angels and demons portrayed in that scene?*

Transition into the lesson with something like—

Kronk is not the brightest bulb in the box; however, at the end he shows us an important truth about spiritual warfare and how to defeat our enemy, the devil: "You're sorta confusing me, so be gone—or however I get rid of you guys." Timothy's church had to deal with spiritual warfare, too; let's look at what Paul told him.

READ IT IN GOD'S WORD

Read aloud to the group (or choose some students to do it for you) 1 Timothy 1:20; 3:6-7; 5:14-15; and 2 Timothy 2:26. Then transition into teaching time with something like—

In 1 and 2 Timothy, Paul refers to Satan four times. But we need to look at what's written about the devil elsewhere in the Bible to better understand Paul's instructions and how we're to fight our enemy. So even though we're studying the Pastoral Epistles, we're going to look at a lot of other passages to help us with the big picture.

Know Your Enemy: Satan's Origin and Identity

DID YOU KNOW?
QUICK FACTS

- **Satan is a fallen angel and NOT equal with God; therefore:**
  - **Satan is not omniscient.**
  - **Satan is not omnipresent.**
  - **Satan is not omnipotent.**
- **The devil appeared in the form of a serpent and tempted Eve.**
- **He's seen most clearly in the Old Testament in Job 1–2.**
- **Satan literally means** *adversary.*
- **Devil literally means** *accuser.*
- **Some of the heavenly hosts followed Satan when he rebelled; they became demons.**
- **There are more than 30 references to** *devil* **in the New Testament.**
- **There are more than 30 references to** *Satan* **in the New Testament.**
- **There are more than 75 references to** *demon* **in the New Testament.**

- It's commonly acknowledged that Isaiah 14:12-14 and Ezekiel 28:11-19 give us further information about the devil's history. You should read them both for greater understanding, but we are going to focus on the passage from Isaiah for our lesson.

> **How you have fallen from heaven, O morning star, son of the dawn! You have been cast down to the earth, you who once laid low the nations! You said in your heart, "I will ascend to heaven; I will raise my throne above the stars of God; I will sit enthroned on the mount of assembly, on the utmost heights of the sacred mountain. I will ascend above the tops of the clouds; I will make myself like the Most High (Isaiah 14:12-14).**

- The phrase "I will" is used five times in those three verses. This shows us that pride is the root of every sin.
- The five references to "I will" are true of Satan's desires and goals; the extreme pride in the statement "I will be like the Most High" correlates with Satan's fall (mentioned in 1 Timothy 3:6).
- Challenge your students to think of one sin that isn't selfish.
- Pride is not only the root of every sin, but it's also at the center of every sinner. Every time you choose to do something that doesn't please God, you're deciding that what you want is more important than what God wants.

• "Pride goes before destruction, a haughty spirit before a fall" (Proverbs 16:18).

ACTIVITY
A DEVIL BY ANY OTHER NAME

You'll need—
• Bibles
• Copies of **A Devil by Any Other Name** (page 77) for each student
• Pen or pencil for each student

Hand out copies of **A Devil by Any Other Name** (page 77) and something to write with to each student. Make sure students have access to Bibles as they work through this sheet. You may even want to break them up into small groups or teams to work on it together. Give them five or 10 minutes to complete it, then go over the correct answers with them:

1. Angel of light—B
2. Enemy—G
3. Roaring lion—G
4. Great dragon—A
5. Ancient serpent—A
6. The evil one—C
7. The tempter—J
8. The prince of this world—D
9. The god of this age—F
10. The ruler of the kingdom of the air—E
11. Father of lies—H
12. Accuser of our brothers—I

Know How Your Enemy Attacks—Satan's Strategy

• "And that they will come to their senses and escape from the trap of the devil, who has taken them captive to do his will" (2 Timothy 2:26).
• Timothy was with Paul when 2 Corinthians was written to the church at Corinth (2 Corinthians 1:1). So he knew the truths about Satan that Paul writes about in this letter.
• "In order that Satan might not outwit us. For we are not unaware of his schemes" (2 Corinthians 2:11).
• We must become aware of Satan's strategies so that he can't fool us. We are learning about his schemes today as we work through this message.
• "The god of this age has blinded the minds of unbelievers, so that they cannot see the light of the gospel of the glory of Christ, who is the image of God" (2 Corinthians 4:4).
• The "god of this age" is our enemy, the devil. We see in the passage that he attacks the minds of unbelievers by blinding them to God's truth.

ILLUSTRATION OPTION
REMEMBER THE TITANS

You'll need—
• *Remember the Titans* (Walt Disney, 2000)
• TV and DVD player
Start 00:58:18 A basketball drops through a hoop.

Stop 00:59:54 Coach Boone says, "I think so."

In this scene Coach Boone (Denzel Washington) talks about the math teacher breaking down the offensive patterns of opposing teams. Get your students into the movie by asking questions like—

- *How can knowing the other team's pattern of plays help the Titans?*
- *How valuable would it be for a football team to have the opposing team's official playbook?*
- *How can knowing our enemy's pattern of attack help us as Christians?*

Know the Word and Resist Your Enemy
- Knowing your enemy's offensive plan is a good way to customize your plan of defense. But you also have to have a good offense to win. Knowing God's truths from his Word will help you win the battle for your mind.
- This isn't just a theoretical idea; we see it in Jesus' life. Jesus used God's Word three times when he was tempted in Matthew 4:1-10. He didn't say, "Give me a minute to get my scroll out and look up a good verse"; he was able to quote Deuteronomy three times because he had memorized God's Word.

LIVE IT IN YOUR WORLD
Give each student a copy of the **My Battle Plan** (page 78) to help them prepare their minds to fight off the enemy, then challenge them to commit to memorizing the verses. It'd be fun to test the students on their Scripture memorization in the coming weeks. You may even want to create some kind of month-long contest and offer prizes to the first student to memorize the first verse, the first one to memorize all of the verses, and so on.

PUT IT IN YOUR HEART
"Submit yourselves, then, to God. Resist the devil, and he will flee from you" (James 4:7).

SMALL GROUP QUESTIONS
1. What's good about pride?
2. What's bad about pride?
3. Is Satan a real being, or is he a metaphorical character created to remind us of the bad part of humans?
4. What did you think or believe about Satan before this lesson?
5. What do you think about Satan now?
6. What one thing stood out for you today that you want to take home and change your life?
7. What do you think about the following C. S. Lewis quote?

> There are two equal and opposite errors into which our race can fall about the devils. One is to disbelieve in their existence. The other is to believe, and to feel an excessive and healthy interest in them. They themselves are equally pleased by both errors, and hail a materialist or a magician with the same delight. —C. S. Lewis, *The Screwtape Letters*

CLOSING PRAYER

A DEVIL BY ANY OTHER NAME

Look up the passages of Scripture and match the references to the different names or descriptions the Bible gives us about Satan. (Two passages are used twice.)

1. Angel of light

2. Enemy

3. Roaring lion

4. Great dragon

5. Ancient serpent

6. The evil one

7. The tempter

8. The prince of this world

9. The god of this age

10. The ruler of the kingdom of the air

11. Father of Lies

12 Accuser of our brothers

A. Revelation 12:9

B. 2 Corinthians 11:14

C. 1 John 5:19

D. John 12:31

E. Ephesians 2:2

F. 2 Corinthians 4:4

G. 1 Peter 5:8

H. John 8:44

I. Rev.12:10

J. 1 Thessalonians 3:5

MY BATTLE PLAN

"How can a young man keep his way pure? By living according to your word…I have hidden your word in my heart that I might not sin against you" (Psalm 119:9, 11).

I acknowledge that the devil is God's enemy and my own, that Christ defeated him on the cross, and that when I resist him, he will flee from me.

I admit that without Christ I can do nothing, that I must renew my mind, and that God wants me to take captive my thoughts captive.

I am in the war of the ages, and I will memorize the five passages given here so that I can win the battle for my mind.

My Orders for Victory
"Submit yourselves, then, to God. Resist the devil, and he will flee from you. Come near to God and he will come near to you" (James 4:7-8).

My Enemy's Plan
"Be self-controlled and alert. Your enemy the devil prowls around like a roaring lion looking for someone to devour" (1 Peter 5:8).

My Attack Plan
"For though we live in the world, we do not wage war as the world does. The weapons we fight with are not the weapons of the world. On the contrary, they have divine power to demolish strongholds. We demolish arguments and every pretension that sets itself up against the knowledge of God, and we take captive every thought to make it obedient to Christ" (2 Corinthians 10:3-5).

My Defense Plan
"Finally, be strong in the Lord and in his mighty power. Put on the full armor of God so that you can take your stand against the devil's schemes" (Ephesians 6:10-11).

"Do not conform any longer to the pattern of this world, but be transformed by the renewing of your mind. Then you will be able to test and approve what God's will is—his good, pleasing and perfect will" (Romans 12:2).

money, money, money!

MONEY, MATERIALISM, AND MORE

session 8

During this session students will—

- **Evaluate some of their attitudes toward money.**
- **Realize that money could become one of the major hindrances to growing in their faith.**

■ THE BIG IDEA

'Ur Hearse won't have a U-Haul® behind it.

Make sure the things you long for are the things that last a long time.

■ BACKGROUND CHECK

According to the Gospels, Jesus said a lot about money. Among the most memorable statements is found in Matthew 6:24: "You cannot serve both God and Money." Since Jesus said a lot about this subject, it shouldn't surprise us that Paul wrote to Timothy about money and materialism.

This passage contains one of the most misquoted verses in the New Testament. 1 Timothy 6:10 says, "For the love of money is a root of all kinds of evil," but more often we hear it quoted this way: "Money is the root of all evil." What a huge difference a few words make!

People have always desired money, and they are rarely satisfied with what they have. There is a story about John D. Rockefeller being asked a simple question while he was the world's richest man: "How much money is enough?" He responded, "One dollar more."

OPENING

Option 1: Four Things in Four Minutes

Open with something like this—

> *If your house was going to be bulldozed in four minutes and you only had time to take four things, which four things would you grab (knowing your family and pets were already safe)?*

It's a classic question, but it's still a good way to get a fresh perspective on all of our stuff and what really matters. Allow a few students to share their responses with the group. Tell the kids what four things you would grab from your house as well.

Now choose a few students from those who just shared and ask them these thought-provoking questions—

- *Why did you choose those four things?*
- *Would those things matter as much to you if you knew you were going to die the next day?*
- *Out of the four items you chose, if you had to have only one, which one would it be?*

Wrap up the discussion and transition into the lesson by saying something like—

> *Today we're going to look at some guidelines that Paul gave Timothy about money and the things of this world.*

Option 2: Movie Clip

Madame Blueberry

You'll need—
- *Veggie Tales: Madame Blueberry* (Big Idea Productions, 1999)
- TV and DVD player

Start 00:08:13 Madame Blueberry says, "Larry, be a dear and bring me some tea."

Stop 00:13:05 The fruits and veggies head to Stuff-Mart, and the scene fades out.

Madame Blueberry (voice of Megan Moore Burns) has a bad case of discontent. In this clip she's just finished complaining about all the nice things her friends have that she doesn't have. Her butlers, Bob (voice of Phil Vischer) and Larry (voice of Mike Nawrocki), are trying to console her when three scallion salesmen from the new Stuff-Mart store appear on her doorstep to make their sales pitch.

After the VeggieTales gang finishes singing "The Stuff-Mart Rap," transition into the lesson with something like—

> *We can laugh at this clip from VeggieTales because it's so true. The economic theory of capitalism works best when discontented consumers buy more new stuff on a regular basis. When it comes to our possessions, Christians tend to be more loyal to our material desires than we are to God's desires. It's easy to believe that if we just had more stuff or the right stuff, we'd be happy. Let's look at what Paul told Timothy.*

READ IT IN GOD'S WORD

"If anyone teaches false doctrines and does not agree to the sound instruction of our Lord Jesus Christ and to godly teaching" (1 Timothy 6:3).

- This is the third time in his letter to Timothy that Paul addresses the topic of false teaching in the church of

Ephesus. The fact that Paul had to cover this issue so many times should make us more aware that even we can be deceived by false teachings.

• If you ever think false teachers can't deceive you, beware! You have to know what the Bible teaches if you are to know if a Bible teacher is right or wrong. Let's see how well you know the Bible with this little quiz.

ACTIVITY
IN THE BIBLE OR NOT?

You'll need—
• Copies of **In the Bible or Not?** quizzes (page 86) for each student
• Pen or pencil for each student

See how well your students recognize the statements and phrases that are found in the Bible. Distribute the **In the Bible or Not?** handout (page 86) and something to write with. Give students four to five minutes to work on it, then ask for a show of hands to see how they voted for each statement. The correct answers are below:

1. Not in the Bible. (The Bible says, "For the love of money is a root of all kinds of evil."—1 Timothy 6:10)
2. Not in the Bible. ("Cleanliness is indeed next to godliness." —John Wesley)
3. In the Bible. (Psalm 137:8-9)
4. Not in the Bible. ("God helps those who help themselves."—Ben Franklin)
5. In the Bible. (Ecclesiastes 8:15)
6. Not in the Bible. (But the Bible does say, "Keep my commands and you will live; guard my teachings as the apple of your eye."—Proverbs 7:2)
7. Not in the Bible. ("But the Lord provided a great fish to swallow Jonah."—Jonah 1:17)
8. In the Bible. (Proverbs 12:1)
9. Not in the Bible. (G.K. Chesterton wrote this.)
10. In the Bible. (Jesus says this in Matthew 6:24.)

• "Godly teaching" implies teaching that leads to godly living or godliness. The relationship between this verse (and the verses that follow) and godliness is important.

• After you hear a Bible lesson you should ask yourself, "What could I do to put that lesson into action?" or, "What should I stop doing to put that lesson into action?"

"He is conceited and understands nothing. He has an unhealthy interest in controversies and quarrels about words that result in envy, strife, malicious talk, evil suspicions and constant friction between men of corrupt mind, who have been robbed of the truth and who think that godliness is a means to financial gain" (1 Timothy 6:4-5).

"They must be silenced, because they are ruining whole households by teaching things they ought not to teach—and that for the sake of dishonest gain" (Titus 1:11).

• False teachers have problems with their hearts (conceited) and their heads (understand nothing). They are more concerned about what people think of them (conceited) and what people might give them (money) than they are concerned about people themselves.

• "Quarrels about words" literally means "word wars." It gives the impression that false teachers argued just to argue.

• "Who think that godliness is a means to financial gain." Now we're getting to the primary theme of this passage. These false teachers were after money, and they thought they could get some by taking advantage of the people of the church.

"But godliness with contentment is great gain. For we brought nothing into the world, and we can take nothing out of it" (1 Timothy 6:6-7).

- Godliness is not the way to gain something. Godliness is the gain itself.
- "With contentment" is the key to this verse. Think of contentment as being satisfied with what you have.
- "'Ur hearse won't have a U-Haul behind it" because you didn't bring anything into this world, and you won't be taking anything with you when you die.
- How are you content? In what areas of life is it good to be content? Should you be content with your spiritual life?

"But if we have food and clothing, we will be content with that" (1 Timothy 6:8).

- Maybe the next time you go shopping for new clothes for the school year, you can make due with one less new shirt or outfit, even if you can afford more. And for *bonus credit* you can give away the money you would have spent on that shirt or outfit to a local homeless shelter.

ACTIVITY
WHAT'S YOUR ROOM WORTH?

You'll need—
- Copies of **What's Your Room Worth?** (page 87) for each student
- Pen or pencil for each student
- Calculators (optional)

Sometimes it's good to sit down and take inventory. Just for a moment, steer your students' focus away from what they don't have and make them think about what they do have. Hand out copies of **What's Your Room Worth?** (page 87) and something to write with. Explain what you're asking them to do, including tallying up the dollar value of their things, and then give them some time to do it. (Use your discretion as to whether or not you should ask a few kids to share their grand totals with everyone. If you have students in your group whose families are suffering financially, it may be best to just have the kids keep their good fortune to themselves.)

After everyone is done with the first part, ask for some responses to these questions—

- *How would your friends and family react if you told them you didn't want anything for your next birthday or for Christmas?*
- *Is that sort of contentment really possible?*

"People who want to get rich fall into temptation and a trap and into many foolish and harmful desires that plunge men into ruin and destruction" (1 Timothy 6:9).

- When people want to get rich, that's known as greed. Greed has always been popular. According to La Fleur's 2001 *World Lottery Almanac,* lottery sales totaled $45 billion in North America, $55 billion in Europe, and $140 billion worldwide just in the year 2000. So the desire to get rich is alive and well in the world today.

QUOTE
"Do not wear yourself out to get rich;
have the wisdom to show restraint.
Cast but a glance at riches, and they are gone,
for they will surely sprout wings
and fly off to the sky like an eagle." —Proverbs 23:4-5

"For the love of money is a root of all kinds of evil. Some people, eager for money, have wandered from the faith and pierced themselves with many griefs" (1 Timothy 6:10).

• We should not love money. Jesus told us that, too. It isn't wrong to have money, but it can be destructive if that's all you desire. When you just want to have more, pretty soon "more" will never be enough.

ACTIVITY
TO BUY OR NOT TO BUY?

You'll need—
• Copies of **To Buy or Not to Buy?** (page 88) for each student
• Pen or pencil for each student

Hand out the **To Buy or Not to Buy?** (page 88) worksheet and something to write with. Begin by saying something like—

Imagine that Bill Gates decided to give away $50 million, and you were the "Grand Prize Winner." Now imagine all the things you could buy with that money—but also realize what you wouldn't be able to buy. For example, you could buy a house but not a home. You could buy college tuition but not an education.

Give the students time to work on their Top 10 lists. When their time is up, ask them to find a partner to share their answers with—they each get 90 seconds to share. They can determine who goes first by seeing who has the longest fingernails. Or you could also ask for volunteers to share their answers with the whole group and just let the students interact with each other in a large-group setting.

"Command those who are rich in this present world not to be arrogant nor to put their hope in wealth, which is so uncertain, but to put their hope in God, who richly provides us with everything for our enjoyment" (1 Timothy 6:17).

• The contrast is clear between this passage and the earlier verses that dealt with money. People who desire wealth are putting their hope in wealth, which they believe will provide them with satisfaction and enjoyment. But it is God alone who can give us all that we need to be content.

"Command them to do good, to be rich in good deeds, and to be generous and willing to share. In this way they will lay up treasure for themselves as a firm foundation for the coming age, so that they may take hold of the life that is truly life" (1 Timothy 6:18-19).

ACTIVITY
MAKING DEPOSITS IN YOUR HEAVENLY BANK ACCOUNT

You'll need—
• Copies of **Making Deposits in Your Heavenly Bank Account** (page 89) for each small group
• Pen or pencil for each small group

Read **The Rich Family in Church** by Eddie Ogan (pages 90-91) to your students. Ask for some reactions to the story. Were they surprised by the family's attitude? Do they think a poor family today wouldn't even realize they were poor? Would a family today make those kinds of sacrifices to help another family in their church? Or families in Africa?

Now divide the students into smaller groups of four or five and give each group a copy of **Making Deposits in Your Heavenly Bank Account** (page 89) and something to write with. Ask them to work together and brainstorm some ideas. After about 10 minutes or so ask a member from each group to share an idea or two with everyone. Then challenge the groups to choose one idea to put into action this week and report back to the youth group what happened during your next meeting.

LIVE IT IN YOUR WORLD

Christians through the centuries have encouraged simplicity as a way of denying ourselves and seeking the things of God. But a life of poverty doesn't make someone more spiritual any more than wealth indicates that someone is more *blessed by God*. Ask your students to consider some ways that simplicity could improve their lives and also how simplicity could make their lives more difficult.

PUT IT IN YOUR HEART

"But godliness with contentment is great gain. For we brought nothing into the world, and we can take nothing out of it" (1 Timothy 6:6-7).

SMALL GROUP QUESTIONS

1. How much money would be enough for you to make per year?
2. Is it wrong for a Christian to own a luxury automobile? Should a Christian own a second house?
3. The old saying goes that if you can't give away something you own, it owns you. What would be three difficult things for you to give away to others?
4. What was Jesus' attitude toward money? What do you base that on?
5. What are some good things that having money can do?
6. Look up Proverbs 28:27. What do you think about that verse?

CLOSING PRAYER

IN THE BIBLE OR NOT?

Circle the correct answer after each statement.

1. Money is the root of all evil.   Not in the Bible.   In the Bible.

2. Cleanliness is next to godliness.   Not in the Bible.   In the Bible.

3. Happy is he who repays you for what you have done to us—he who seizes your infants and dashes them against the rocks.   Not in the Bible.   In the Bible.

4. God helps those who help themselves.   Not in the Bible.   In the Bible.

5. Nothing is better for a man under the sun than to eat and drink and be glad.   Not in the Bible.   In the Bible.

6. Guard it as the apple of your eye.   Not in the Bible.   In the Bible.

7. Jonah was swallowed by a whale.   Not in the Bible.   In the Bible.

8. Whoever loves discipline loves knowledge, but he who hates correction is stupid.   Not in the Bible.   In the Bible.

9. A man who has faith must be prepared not only to be a martyr, but to be a fool.   Not in the Bible.   In the Bible.

10. You cannot serve both God and Money.   Not in the Bible.   In the Bible.

WHAT'S YOUR ROOM WORTH?

Name three things you would change or improve about your bedroom.

1. _____

2. _____

3. _____

Estimate the cost of all the items in your bedroom. Include clothes, computer, furniture, CDs, decorations, and anything else. (Use the back of this handout if you need more room!)

_____

_____

_____

_____

_____

_____

_____

_____

_____

_____

_____

_____

Total $: _____

TO BUY OR NOT TO BUY?

List the top 10 things you could buy with $50 million:

1. _____

2. _____

3. _____

4. _____

5. _____

6. _____

7. _____

8. _____

9. _____

10. _____

List the top 10 things you could not buy with $50 million:

1. _____

2. _____

3. _____

4. _____

5. _____

6. _____

7. _____

8. _____

9. _____

10. _____

MAKING DEPOSITS IN YOUR HEAVENLY BANK ACCOUNT

I can start sharing with those in need by—

Physically:

Start doing: _____

_____

_____

Stop doing: _____

_____

_____

Individually:

Start doing: _____

_____

_____

Stop doing: _____

_____

_____

As a youth group or church:

Start doing: _____

_____

_____

Stop doing: _____

_____

_____

THE RICH FAMILY IN CHURCH

by Eddie Ogan

I'll never forget Easter 1946. I was 14, my little sister Ocy was 12, and my older sister Darlene 16. We lived at home with our mother, and the four of us knew what it was to do without many things. My dad had died five years before, leaving Mom with seven school kids to raise and no money.

By 1946 my older sisters were married, and my brothers had left home. A month before Easter the pastor of our church announced that a special Easter offering would be taken to help a poor family. He asked everyone to save and give sacrificially.

When we got home, we talked about what we could do. We decided to buy 50 pounds of potatoes and live on them for a month. This would allow us to save $20 of our grocery money for the offering. Then we thought that if we kept our electric lights turned out as much as possible and didn't listen to the radio, we'd save money on that month's electric bill. Darlene got as many house and yard cleaning jobs as possible, and both of us baby-sat for everyone we could. For 15 cents we could buy enough cotton loops to make three pot holders to sell for $1. We made $20 on pot holders. That month was one of the best of our lives.

Every day we counted the money to see how much we had saved. At night we'd sit in the dark and talk about how the poor family was going to enjoy having the money the church would give them. We had about 80 people in church, so we figured that whatever amount of money we had to give, the offering would surely be 20 times that much. After all, every Sunday the pastor had reminded everyone to save for the sacrificial offering.

The day before Easter, Ocy and I walked to the grocery store and got the manager to give us three crisp $20 bills and one $10 bill for all our change.

We ran all the way home to show Mom and Darlene. We had never had so much money before.

That night we were so excited we could hardly sleep. We didn't care that we wouldn't have new clothes for Easter; we had $70 for the sacrificial offering.

We could hardly wait to get to church! On Sunday morning rain was pouring. We didn't own an umbrella, and the church was over a mile from our home, but it didn't seem to matter how wet we got. Darlene had cardboard in her shoes to fill the holes. The cardboard came apart, and her feet got wet.

But we sat in church proudly. I heard some teenagers talking about the Smith girls having on their old dresses. I looked at them in their new clothes, and I felt rich.

When the sacrificial offering was taken, we were sitting in the second row from the front. Mom put in the $10 bill, and each of us kids put in a $20.

As we walked home after church, we sang all the way. At lunch Mom had a surprise for us. She had bought a dozen eggs, and we had boiled Easter eggs with our fried potatoes! Late that afternoon the minister drove up in his car. Mom went to the door, talked with him for a moment, and then came back with an envelope in her hand. We asked what it was, but she didn't say a word. She opened the envelope and out fell a bunch of money. There were three crisp $20 bills, one $10 bill, and 17 $1 bills.

Mom put the money back in the envelope. We didn't talk, just sat and stared at the floor. We had gone from feeling like millionaires to feeling like poor white trash. We kids had such a happy life that we felt sorry for anyone who didn't have our mom and dad for parents and a house full of brothers and sisters and other kids visiting constantly. We thought it was fun to share silverware and see whether we got the spoon or the fork that night.

We had two knives that we passed around to whoever needed them. I knew we didn't have a lot of things that other people had, but I'd never thought we were poor.

That Easter day I found out we were. The minister had brought us the money for the poor family, so we must be poor. I didn't like being poor. I looked at my dress and worn-out shoes and felt so ashamed—I didn't even want to go back to church. Everyone there probably already knew we were poor!

I thought about school. I was in the ninth grade and at the top of my class of over 100 students. I wondered if the kids at school knew that we were poor. I decided that I could quit school since I had finished the eighth grade. That was all the law required at that time. We sat in silence for a long time. Then it got dark, and we went to bed. All that week we girls went to school and came home, and no one talked much. Finally, on Saturday Mom asked us what we wanted to do with the money. What did poor people do with money? We didn't know. We'd never known we were poor. We didn't want to go to church on Sunday, but Mom said we had to. Although it was a sunny day, we didn't talk on the way.

Mom started to sing, but no one joined in, and she only sang one verse. At church we had a missionary speaker. He talked about how churches in Africa made buildings out of sun-dried bricks, but they needed money to buy roofs. He said $100 would put a roof on a church. The minister said, "Can't we all sacrifice to help these poor people?" We looked at each other and smiled for the first time in a week.

Mom reached into her purse and pulled out the envelope. She passed it to Darlene. Darlene gave it to me, and I handed it to Ocy. Ocy put it in the offering.

When the offering was counted, the minister announced that it was a little over $100. The missionary was excited. He hadn't expected such a large offering from our small church. He said, "You must have some rich people in this church."

Suddenly it struck us! We had given $87 of that "little over $100."

We were the rich family in the church! Hadn't the missionary said so? From that day on I've never been poor again. I've always remembered how rich I am because I have Jesus! (*Used with the permission of Eddie Ogan.*)

From Creative Bible Lessons in 1 & 2 Timothy and Titus by Len Evans. Permission to reproduce this page granted only for use in buyer's own youth group. ©2004 by Youth Specialties. www.YouthSpecialties.com

passing the torch of faith

HELPING OTHERS AS OTHERS HAVE HELPED YOU

session 9

During this session students will—

- Realize that their faith has been handed down to them and that they must pass it on to others.
- Evaluate which parts of their faith have been tainted by their own culture.

◼ THE BIG IDEA

As Christians we must not only believe, but we must also believe the right things. In order to maintain a biblical faith you must have received a biblical faith from someone. To continue a biblical faith you must pass it on to others.

◼ BACKGROUND CHECK

It shouldn't surprise us that 2 Timothy continues to deal with false teachers. After all, nearly the entire book of 1 Timothy focuses on the fact that false teachers were weak in the faith—if they had any faith at all—and the way to confront and conquer the lies and false teachers was to be strong in the grace that is in Christ Jesus.

OPENING
Option 1: Everyone's Out to Get You!

You'll need—
- Plastic sandwich bags (the kind that zip closed), one for each player
- A raw egg for each bag
- Duct tape

Before you start the game you should determine the playing area's perimeter. It should be large enough to allow players to make some evasive maneuvers to avoid getting caught but not so open that people can just run away from each other and the game never ends. And as participants are eliminated, you should call a quick time out and shrink the boundaries to keep it challenging.

Create teams of two to four players and instruct each team to stand together. For each player, put a raw egg into a sandwich bag and seal it up. Then use duct tape to attach the baggie to the person's back. After you've assigned the teams and everyone has an egg-filled bag taped to their backs, give the instructions:

- *You play as a team, so look out for each other.*
- *Stay in the designated area—if you leave the area, you are out.*
- *Your job is to break the eggs on the backs of your opponents by using your hand while protecting your own egg so it doesn't get broken.*
- *Do not pull the bag off an opponent's back; if you do, you are out.*
- *Once your egg is broken, you are out.*
- *The last team with a player left in the game—AND with an intact egg in the bag on their back—is the winning team.*

Transition to the lesson with something like this—

People are often out to get you, and you don't stand a chance if you have to face them alone. Being with other people doesn't guarantee a victory, but you have a better chance of survival when you stand together as a group.

Option 2: Telephone with a Twist
Here's a classic party game that has been modified. The leader arranges everyone in the group to sit in a circle or stand in a line. (If you have a large group, select seven to 10 students to do this in front of everyone.) The leader whispers a sentence into the first student's ear one time, and then each student repeats what they heard (or think they heard) into the ear of the next person and on down the line until the last person must repeat the sentence out loud.

Here are two sample sentences you can use to get the game started:

1. Al and Ruth dated during high school; he went to college, she got a job, they got married, and they lived happily ever after.

2. Dr. Pepper sips soda through a straw while wearing his stethoscope and examining the conditions of his patient patients.

Start the game by whispering to the first student and have the last person only say the sentence out loud as they heard it. Typically the end result is very different from the original sentence. Do that once or twice and then tell them you are going to do one last round. However, this time it will be a little different.

Before the game, you should copy the following instructions and sentences onto a piece of paper (or you can also copy this page from the book and just cut out the box below):

(Whisper the sentence below into the ear of the next person and then hand them this piece of paper.)
God loves us, and he tells us about his love in the Bible. Good teachers help us better understand the Bible and more about God's love in a proper way.

Now whisper the sentence from your sheet of paper into the first person's ear, making sure they see that you're reading it from the paper. Hand them the paper after you're finished reading the sentence to them. They should do likewise as they whisper into the next player's ear and on down the line until the last person reads it aloud to the whole group.

Now transition into the lesson with something like this—

Not surprisingly, it was much easier to repeat the message to the person next to us when it was written down. It helped us to pass on the original message and not get things confused. Paul commanded Timothy to do something similar with a much more important message. That message is found in 2 Timothy 2:1-7.

READ IT IN GOD'S WORD
"You then, my son, be strong in the grace that is in Christ Jesus" (2 Timothy 2:1).

• "You then" refers to the previous chapter but especially 2 Timothy 1:13-18
• 2 Timothy 1:13-14—Follow the pattern I showed you and taught you.
• 2 Timothy 1:15—These two didn't follow that pattern.
• 2 Timothy 1:16-18—Onesiphorus did follow that same pattern; be like him.
• Paul is referring to the command he gave in 2 Timothy 1:13 and the two possible outcomes of obeying or disobeying it. Paul wants Timothy to follow the example of Onesiphorus. Timothy knew very well the faithfulness of Onesiphorus (2 Timothy 1:18).
• "My son"—Timothy knew how Paul felt about him and that he was regarded as his son in the faith. Paul called Timothy "my son" here for two reasons:
   • To remind the church, the people who also received this letter, that Paul endorsed Timothy and his ministry.
   • To give Timothy one more reason to follow through with his duty. Timothy would want to live and please Paul and God with his assignment.
• Timothy represented Paul and his ministry, but more importantly he represented Christ, and so should we.

"Be strong in the grace that is in Christ Jesus" (2 Timothy 2:1).

• Timothy was not told to "try harder"; he was told to "stop trying and rely upon God's grace through Jesus Christ." Timothy's strength was to come from grace, which came from Christ.
• The joy of this is that your faith and your ability to pass on your faith are not dependent totally on your strength but on Christ's strength (Philippians 4:13; Galatians 2:20).
• Whatever you do, do it in grace.

"And the things you have heard me say in the presence of many witnesses entrust to reliable men who will also be qualified to teach others" (2 Timothy 2:2).

• In 2 Timothy 1:13, Paul writes, "What you heard from me, keep as the pattern of sound teaching, with faith and love in Christ Jesus."

• Christianity has always offered the same message but through different messengers. The important part is not who is delivering the message of salvation and spiritual growth but that the message of salvation and spiritual growth is being delivered.

• Here the Greek word translated as *men* usually means "human beings." If Paul wanted to ensure that no women were involved, he could have used the word that means exclusively "for men."

• As a leader Paul was not a one-man band; he was the conductor of an orchestra. He not only involved others in his work, but his work was also better with others involved. Both the one-man band and the orchestra make music, but you'll probably never buy the CD of a one-man band.

FOR YOUR INFORMATION
WOMEN WORKERS IN PAUL'S WORK
• Euodia and Syntyche were "fellow workers" in Philippi (Philippians 4:2-3).

• Priscilla and her husband, Aquila, explained to Apollos "the way of God more adequately," and the church met in their home (Acts 18:24-26 and 1 Corinthians 16:19).

• Phoebe was a servant of the church in Cenchrea, and Paul called her a great help to himself (Romans 16:1-2).

• Tryphena and Tryphosa and Persis "worked very hard in the Lord" with Paul (Romans 16:12).

• Lydia was the first convert in Europe, and she supported the church in Philippi (Acts 16:11-15, 40).

ACTIVITY
Passing the Torch of Faith

You'll need—
• Copies of **Passing the Torch of Faith** (page 98) for each student
• Pen or pencil for each student

Hand out copies of **Passing the Torch of Faith** (page 98) and something to write with. Give your students about five minutes to go over the handout on their own, and then they should discuss it as a group. Ask if any student was able to diagram his spiritual family tree. Choose a student whose tree has many *branches* and invite her to come forward and draw it again on a chalkboard or a spot where the whole group can see it.

• Paul writes, "Do your best to come to me quickly" in 2 Timothy 4:9, so it was very likely that Timothy would be leaving soon to reach Paul before winter (2 Timothy 4:21). In light of this, Timothy didn't have time to start a leadership program where he'd train others to take over his responsibilities in his absence. So it would seem that Timothy, following the example of Paul, had already been training others to pass on the torch of faith. And they would then be able to pass it on to even more people.

"Endure hardship with us like a good soldier of Christ Jesus. No one serving as a soldier gets involved in civilian affairs—he wants to please his commanding officer" (2 Timothy 2:3-4).

• "Endure hardship"—Life is full of struggles, but this particular hardship Paul mentions relates to working to advance God's ministry. Hardships are going to happen. You must learn to endure them and not bother trying to escape them.

ILLUSTRATION
Play the Rich Mullins song "Bound to Come Some Trouble" (on two albums: *Never Picture Perfect* and *Songs 2.*) You can play it during the portion of the lesson about hardships, or you can close your meeting while playing this song in the background. Ask students to pray, think, and reflect about what this song is saying.

- We are encouraged to be not just soldiers but good soldiers. What does it take to be a good soldier?
- Soldiers focus on obeying the orders of their commanding officer. What are you focused on doing?

"Similarly, if anyone competes as an athlete, he does not receive the victor's crown unless he competes according to the rules" (2 Timothy 2:5).

- Historians tell us that some of the Olympic-type games that were held during Paul's time required strict training for 10 months before the event. So the rules of the games included requirements for training beforehand.
- The important thing is that the athletes followed the rules. If they didn't train for the required 10 months, they were disqualified before they competed. And if they broke the rules during the competition, they were also disqualified. Either way, they didn't want to be disqualified.
- The victor's crown was the greatest of awards given in those days. It was as valuable as a gold medal, and though it wouldn't last, the glory of the victory lasted forever.

"The hardworking farmer should be the first to receive a share of the crops" (2 Timothy 2:6).

- Farmers have to work hard to get good crops, yet they still have no control over the results (due to weather conditions, soil quality, weeds, pests, and so on).
- Farmers' "share of the crop" refers to the reward for their labors, which also means food and survival for their families.

"Reflect on what I am saying, for the Lord will give you insight into all this" (2 Timothy 2:7).

- Jesus said in John 14:26, "But the Counselor, the Holy Spirit, whom the Father will send in my name, will teach you all things and will remind you of everything I have said to you." The Holy Spirit helps us to better understand God's Word.
- There is a connection between reflection and revelation. Revelation is used to explain the truths that God shares with us. *Direct revelation* is the phrase theologians use regarding how God shares his truth with believers through the Word. *General revelation* is the phrase theologians use regarding how God shares his truth with everyone throughout the world.

LIVE IT IN YOUR WORLD

ACTIVITY
AM I A SOLDIER, ATHLETE, OR FARMER?

You'll need—
- Copies of **Am I a Soldier, Athlete, or Farmer?** (page 99) for each student
- Pen or pencil for each student

Paul paints three portraits using different professions to give us one overall theme about endurance and hardships. Hand out the **Am I a Soldier, Athlete, or Farmer?** (page 99) pages and something to write with. Give your students some time to reflect and fill them out. Then ask for a show of hands to indicate how many students chose soldier, how many chose athlete, and how many chose farmer. Continue the discussion by picking a few kids from each *professional group* to share their responses to the questions on the page.

PUT IT IN YOUR HEART

"And the things you have heard me say in the presence of many witnesses entrust to reliable men who will also be qualified to teach others" (2 Timothy 2:2).

SMALL GROUP QUESTIONS

1. Why do you feel uncomfortable trying to pass on your faith?
2. Who has invested their lives into yours and made your life different?
3. Why is it hard to share our feelings with everyone through these kinds of questions?
4. Do you find it difficult to slow down and reflect upon what God may or may not be telling you?
5. How do you know the difference between God talking to you and a reaction to some bad pizza from the night before?
6. What can you do this next week to put this lesson into action?
7. Name the most difficult experience in your life so far. How scared were you while it was going on?
8. What are some practical steps you can take to endure hardship?

CLOSING PRAYER

PASSING THE TORCH OF FAITH

"And the things you have heard me say in the presence of many witnesses entrust to reliable men who will also be qualified to teach others" (2 Timothy 2:2).

1. Christians function in community—we need others, and others need us (even leaders). How many generations or levels of teachers do you see in 2 Timothy 2:2?

Who is my Paul?

2. Which person (or people) invested in my faith and helped me to know what a strong Christian should look like?

3. What do I admire about that person?

4. Why has he been able to help me?

5. Which of those characteristics can I begin to work on so that others will one day say that about me?

Who is my Timothy?

6. Who am I able to encourage in her faith? (I might not be her leader, but I am further along in my spiritual journey than they are. And if you don't have a "Timothy," begin praying for God to bring someone into your life so you can help and encourage him in his faith.)

Who are my reliable people?

7. Who am I helping to become a leader?

8. If God allows the world to continue for another 100 years, what can you do today that could influence someone 100 years from now?

Dwight L. Moody was the greatest evangelist of the 1800s. He preached across America and in Europe to over 100 million people. He founded the Moody Bible Institute, which still exists as a college today, and wrote numerous books. He became a Christian, however, because of his Sunday school teacher—Edward Kimball—who visited the young D. L. Moody while he was working at a shoe store. In the back of that store Moody became a Christian.

9. Can you trace your spiritual family tree? (If so, draw it here.)

AM I A SOLDIER, ATHLETE, OR FARMER?

1. Which of these three professions best reflects you—soldier, athlete, or farmer?

2. Why did you pick that one?

3. What does it take to be good at your chosen profession?

4. What's the motivation of that professional?

5. Who are those professionals accountable to for their actions and attitudes?

6. What can you learn from that profession to help you put your faith into action?

overcoming the opposition

YOUR DESIRES AND YOUR DEFENSE

session 10

During this session students will—

- **Understand that they are not alone in their struggle to live right.**
- **Develop a personalized way to resist the temptations they face.**

■ **THE BIG IDEA**

If you want to consistently succeed, you'll need a consistent plan, and then you'll need to act on that plan.

■ **BACKGROUND CHECK**

Paul understood what it meant to struggle with sin and be tempted. Read Romans 7:14-20 for more details about Paul's struggle with sin and incorporate that into the lesson, too. He shared this with Timothy in his earlier letter: "Here is a trustworthy saying that deserves full acceptance: Christ Jesus came into the world to save sinners—of whom I am the worst" (1 Timothy 1:15).

Paul also understood how to overcome sin: "No temptation has seized you except what is common to man. And God is faithful; he will not let you be tempted beyond what you can bear. But when you are tempted, he will also provide a way out so that you can stand up under it" (1 Corinthians 10:13).

OPENING
Option 1: Ox·y·mo·ron

You'll need—
• Blank sheet of paper for each team
• Pen or pencil for each team
• An oxymoronic prize for the winner

Divide students into teams of three to five players. Explain what an oxymoron is—a combination of contradictory or incongruous words—and share some examples, such as "military intelligence," "jumbo shrimp," "liquid paper," or "poor Bill Gates."

Give each team a pen, a piece of paper, and four minutes to list as many oxymorons as they can. The winning team could win an oxymoronic prize such as fat-free chips, decaffeinated coffee, or sugar-free candy.

Transition by saying something like—

There are some apparent oxymorons in the Christian faith, meaning they seem to contradict each other—but they really don't. For example, the biggest oxymoron is that God became man and was fully God and fully man at the same time!

A. W. Tozer writes that a Christian "empties himself in order to be full, admits he is wrong so he can be declared right, goes down in order to get up, is strongest when he is weakest, richest when he is poorest, and happiest when he feels worst. He dies so he can live, forsakes in order to have, gives away so he can keep, sees the invisible, hears the inaudible, and knows that which passes knowledge" (from The Root of Righteousness, *page 156).*

In the same way, in order to resist temptation and be truly free, you must submit to boundaries and limits. Paul gave Timothy some ideas on how he could best resist his sinful desires by preparing a good defense against them.

Option 2: Mapping the Journey—Getting There from Here

You'll need—
• Copies of **Interstates Across the U.S.A.** (page 106) for each student
• Road atlases for students to share
• Blank paper for each student
• Pen or pencil for each student

Hand out copies of **Interstates Across the U.S.A.** (page 106) Ask students to look at their maps and plan the route for a trip from Chicago, Illinois, to San Antonio, Texas, and then on to Montgomery, Alabama. Ask them to look for the best route from Chicago to Montgomery. (The answer is I-65 South. It's the easiest route because you stay on I-65 for the entire drive.)

Transition with something like this—

When you look at a map, it's fairly easy to see the best route to your destination. In the same way, we need to look for the best way to run from temptation. Human desire toward sin is no different now than it was at the beginning of time, so we should listen to what Paul writes to Timothy regarding how to handle his desires.

READ IT IN GOD'S WORD

"Flee the evil desires of youth" (2 Timothy 2:22).

• A simple formula for fighting off desires that can hinder us or hurt people around us—FLEE!
• Temptation is common to everyone, and temptation is everywhere. "No temptation has seized you except what is common to man. And God is faithful; he will not let you be tempted beyond what you can bear. But when you are tempted, he will also provide a way out so that you can stand up under it" (1 Corinthians 10:13).
• The word *flee* is from the Greek word *phueg*. It's the root word for fugitive. A fugitive is constantly on the run. In the same way, we should constantly run away from our sinful desires.
• The command to flee implies that what's needed is a continual flight from the evil desires that tempted Timothy. He was always to run away from the evil desires that were in his heart. When he heard this command, Timothy would have thought of Joseph running from temptation when he ran away from Potiphar's wife in Genesis 39:1-12. Our response to temptation should also be that dramatic. We need to develop an escape route.
• "Desires of youth" implies sexual temptations but also pride, impatience, selfishness, greed, and others.

ACTIVITY
EVACUATION ROUTE TO SAFETY

You'll need—
• Copies of **Evacuation Route to Safety** (page 107) for each student
• Pen or pencil for each student
• Bibles

Hurricanes can destroy everything in their paths, which is why people who live where a hurricane is projected to hit are strongly encouraged to leave. In the same way, we're encouraged to flee from temptation. God will provide a way of escape for you when you face temptation, but you have to be ready. 1 Corinthians 10:13 says, "No temptation has seized you except what is common to man. And God is faithful; he will not let you be tempted beyond what you can bear. But when you are tempted, he will also provide a way out so that you can stand up under it."

Here is a worksheet to help you think about what things tempt you and how you might run from those temptations with God's help.

Hand out the **Evacuation Route to Safety** pages (page 107) and something to write with, then give the students some time to reflect and answer the questions as honestly as they can. Assure them that they won't have to share their answers if they don't want to. After 10 minutes or so discuss the questions and share your own responses regarding a particular temptation if there are no student volunteers. Tell them what your evacuation route is should you be tempted in any of your weak areas.

End this part of the lesson by saying something like—

If we don't follow our escape routes, we will fall into sin instead of fleeing from it. And the consequences of bad choices can last a lifetime.

QUOTE

"In our members there is a slumbering inclination toward desire which is both sudden and fierce. Satan does not here fill us with hatred of God, but with forgetfulness of God." —Dietrich Bonhoeffer

"And pursue righteousness, faith, love and peace" (2 Timothy 2:22).

• James tells us, "Submit yourselves, then, to God. Resist the devil, and he will flee from you. Come near to God and he will come near to you" (4:7-8).
• In *The Message*, Eugene Peterson clearly shows what Paul is saying when he translates the first part of 2 Timothy 2:22 as, "Run away from infantile indulgence. Run after mature righteousness." It's not enough to just run away from bad—we must also run toward good.
• The word *pursue* literally means to "keep on pursuing," so we should never stop going after the good Paul shows us. There are no breaks when it comes to obeying God.
• Here peace refers to peace between people and not peace between nations.

"Along with those who call on the Lord out of a pure heart" (2 Timothy 2:22).

• Paul is telling Timothy that it isn't good for him to function alone; others have to help him.
• We have to establish patterns that reflect and reinforce our faith as we live our faith with others. We must make efforts to not forget the important things and allow others to hold us accountable for our attitudes and actions.

QUOTE

"Contrary to much of our current thinking about the importance of powerful youth ministries to the lifelong spiritual development of future adults, research proves otherwise: a teenager who attends a church's worship service on a regular basis and does not attend youth group is more likely to continue to attend church worship services as an adult than a teen who is active in youth group but doesn't attend worship services with other age groups."—Mark Oestreicher (from *The Emerging Church*, p. 33)

ACTIVITY
WHAT IS THE CHURCH?

You'll need—
• Copies of **What Is the Church?** (page 108) for each student
• Pen or pencil for each student

Pass out the **What Is the Church?** pages (page 108). Have the students follow the instructions on the sheet, and after they are done working, explain to them that the church is more about the believers who attend than it is about the place where they gather.

Ask different students to explain their drawings and share their answers after they have finished. Or they can share these in small groups instead.

ACTIVITY
ALONG FOR THE RIDE

You'll need—
• Copies of **Along for the Ride** (page 109) for each student
• Pen or pencil for each student

Read these instructions to your students after you've passed out the **Along for the Ride** sheets (page 109) and something to write with—

1. Imagine that you are driving in your brand-new SUV with your five closest friends. List your five closest friends on the sheet.

2. Now that you've completed your list, think about how spiritually mature your friends are compared to you. Next write the phrase "stronger spiritually, equal spiritually, or weaker spiritually" on the lines to the right of their names.

3. If you have four or five friends who are spiritually stronger than you, you should befriend others who are spiritually weaker so you can help them. Can you think of anybody like this?

If you have four or five friends who are your spiritual equals, you should find others who are spiritually stronger than you so they can challenge you to grow. Can you think of someone who is spiritually stronger than you and who might also be willing to mentor you on a regular basis?

And if you have four or five friends who are spiritually weaker than you, you should find more friends who can walk beside you in your spiritual journey.

"Don't have anything to do with foolish and stupid arguments, because you know they produce quarrels. And the Lord's servant must not quarrel; instead, he must be kind to everyone, able to teach, not resentful" (2 Timothy 2:23-24).

• False teachers tried to bait Timothy into talking about things that really didn't matter. Paul wanted Timothy to focus on what was important while he was explaining and defending the truth, not just argue. It's a matter of the heart for believers to be "kind to everyone," even those who oppose us.

• In Old Testament times Jews who were destitute or in debt could become servants to fellow Jews. The law required that they be treated well and that after six years of service they were set free.

• The law also allowed a servant to become a bond servant. A bond servant could choose to stay with his master because a relationship had developed, and the servant had been treated so well that he wanted to become the master's bond servant for life! (The bond servant gave up all his rights in order to serve his master and spend his life pleasing him.)

• The servant could become a bond servant by participating in a public ceremony with witnesses. A sharp instrument would be used to pierce a hole in the servant's ear, and by doing so it would be a permanent and public declaration that their life was no longer theirs but belonged to their master (Exodus 21:5-6).

• Jesus was pierced so that we could be freed from our bondage to sin. Once we've been freed, we need to choose to become his bond servant and surrender our total will to his. Moses (Joshua 14:7), David (Psalm 89:3), and Elijah (2 Kings 10:10) were each called "servants of the Lord." What would it take in your life for you to be known as a servant of the Lord?

"Those who oppose him he must gently instruct, in the hope that God will grant them repentance leading them to a knowledge of the truth, and that they will come to their senses and escape from the trap of the devil, who has taken them captive to do his will" (2 Timothy 2:25-26).

• Through all of this Timothy still has to "gently instruct" those who oppose him. Paul's ultimate hope for change is not in Timothy's ability to follow his guidelines but in God's ability to bring these people to repentance. They didn't know the truth yet, but Paul hoped that they would one day understand the truth and realize the error of their ways.

• Escaping from the devil's trap implies that they were already trapped. The devil has always wanted to trap believers into believing lies about God and God's faithfulness. We don't have to deny God to accomplish the devil's will—as long as we aren't fully devoted to God, the devil's work is being done; for when we fail to do God's will, we are essentially doing the devil's will.

LIVE IT IN YOUR WORLD

Encourage your students to take home their Evacuation Route to Safety sheets as a reminder regarding the areas of their life where they are tempted. Encourage them to work on memorizing the Scripture(s) that will help them flee those temptations in the future.

PUT IT IN YOUR HEART

"Flee the evil desires of youth, and pursue righteousness, faith, love and peace, along with those who call on the Lord out of a pure heart" (2 Timothy 2:22).

SMALL GROUP QUESTIONS

1. If you had to run in a race, would you rather run a 40-yard dash, a 4 x 40 relay race, or a marathon?
2. Who is the godliest student you know?
3. What is it about this person that made you choose him?
4. How hard is it for you to not get angry over little things?

CLOSING PRAYER

INTERSTATES ACROSS THE U.S.A.

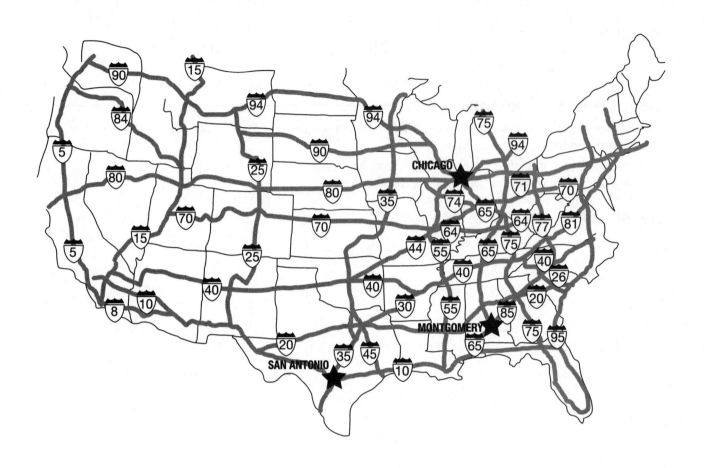

EVACUATION ROUTE TO SAFETY

"How can a young man keep his way pure? By living according to your word...
I have hidden your word in my heart that I might not sin against you" (Psalm 119:9, 11).

Do you have an evacuation route planned for when temptation comes your way?

1. What is the biggest temptation in your life?

_____

2. How often do you give in to this temptation?

_____

3. What leads up to your giving in to this temptation?

_____

4. How can you avoid being near this temptation?

_____

5. Who can you talk to about this temptation so she can help you?

_____

6. What verse can you memorize to think about when you are tempted by this?

_____

Lust—"Each of you should learn to control his own body in a way that is holy and honorable, not in passionate lust like the heathen, who do not know God" (1 Thessalonians 4:4-5).

Greed—"A greedy man stirs up dissension, but he who trusts in the Lord will prosper" (Proverbs 28:25).

Pride—"Young men, in the same way be submissive to those who are older. All of you, clothe yourselves with humility toward one another, because, 'God opposes the proud but gives grace to the humble'" (1 Peter 5:5).

Envy—"Let us not become conceited, provoking and envying each other" (Galatians 5:26).

Lying—"Keep your tongue from evil and your lips from speaking lies" (Psalm 34:13).

Gossip—"A gossip betrays a confidence, but a trustworthy man keeps a secret" (Proverbs 11:13).

Stealing—"'Do not steal. Do not lie. Do not deceive one another'" (Leviticus 19:11).

Anger—"'In your anger do not sin': Do not let the sun go down while you are still angry" (Ephesians 4:26).

Sexual Sin—"But among you there must not be even a hint of sexual immorality, or of any kind of impurity, or of greed, because these are improper for God's holy people" (Ephesians 5:3).

WHAT IS THE CHURCH?

1. Draw the Church.

2. Draw four items that represent the Church to you.

3. If you could create an ideal church, what would be the five most important things about it?

_____

_____

4. What's the difference between going to church and being the Church?

_____

_____

5. What two things would you change about your own church?

_____

_____

ALONG FOR THE RIDE

1. _____   _____

2. _____   _____

3. _____   _____

4. _____   _____

5. _____   _____

the b-i-b-l-e

KNOW THE WORD AND YOUR WORK

During this session students will—

- Realize how special it is to have a personal copy of the Bible.
- Be challenged to start reading the Bible in a new way.

■ THE BIG IDEA

We shouldn't take the Bible for granted. People risked their lives so that every person could own a copy of it written in their own language. It's an amazing, timeless book that still holds truths that are relevant in our lives today, so we should make time to read the Bible and try to apply it to our lives.

■ BACKGROUND CHECK

THE BIBLE AT A GLANCE

The Old Testament points toward Christ and the cross. The New Testament points toward Christ, the cross, and Christ's kingdom and future glory. The entire Bible revolves around Jesus.

To show the contrast between the false teachers and Timothy, you should spend some time reviewing the verses about false teachers that you already covered in the previous sessions. Then read the following passages so you'll be familiar with the different verses where the Bible talks about itself.

Deuteronomy 11:18	Jeremiah 15:16	Romans 15:4	1 Peter 2:2
Ezra 7:10	Matthew 22:29	Ephesians 6:17	2 Peter 1:19
Psalm 19:7	Matthew 24:35	Colossians 3:16	2 Peter 1:20-21
Psalm 119:9-11	Acts 17:11	Hebrews 4:12	1 John 5:13

THE BIBLE AT A GLANCE

According to Wycliffe Bible Translators, "Only 5% of the world's language groups have access to the entire Bible! Roughly 30% of the language groups only have part of the Bible in their language... that leaves about 65% of the world's language groups that don't know God 'speaks' their language."

If you have a Bible written in the same language you speak, you possess a precious treasure that others would die for. If you own a Bible but don't read it, then you have no advantage over the man who doesn't have a Bible; or the man who does, but can't read it. Are you making good use of your treasure?

OPENING
Option 1: Bible Numbers

You'll need—
- Copies of **Bible Numbers** (page 118) for each student
- Pen or pencil for each student
- Some kind of food prize (optional)

Hand out copies of **Bible Numbers** (page 118) and something to write with to each student. Introduce the activity by saying something like—

Today we're going to talk about the Bible and why it's a unique book among all books. Fill in the blanks in the paragraph, which give information about the Bible and about the ongoing work to translate the Bible into different languages.

Give them time to read through the paragraph and fill in the blanks. Turn it into a timed contest if you like and give a prize for the first one to finish with all the right answers.

Here is the paragraph with the correct numbers inserted:

The Bible was written over 1,500 hundred years, by more than 40 men from very different walks of life. It was written under many different circumstances on 3 different continents and in 3 different languages. The writers had different purposes for writing, and they addressed a multitude of issues. Yet there is unity. That unity is organized around one theme: God's redemption of people and all of creation. The Bible, as we know it, is comprised of 66 different books, with 39 in the Old Testament and 27 in the New Testament. In 1999, Wycliffe Translators reported that of the 6,809 languages in the world, only 405 had an entire Bible translation in their own language; 1,034 had an adequate New Testament; 883 had some Scripture in their own language, there were 1,500 languages being translated at that time; and over 3,000 different languages didn't have a copy of God's Word (from Patrick Johnstone's book *Operation World*).

Transition to the next part of the lesson with something like this—

Today we are going to look at why the Bible is our reliable source for the truth.

Option 2: Which Truth Do You Trust?
Divide your students into smaller groups of five or six. Then display the list below so everyone can see it. You may wish to explain that *The Book of Mormon* is the sacred text for the Church of Jesus Christ of Latter Day Saints (or the Mormon Church) and *The Bhagavad-Gita* is the sacred text for the International Society for Krishna Consciousness (or Hare Krishnas).

USA Today
The Bible
The Book of Mormon
The Bhagavad-Gita
CNN
The New York Times
FoxNews Channel
Time Magazine
Mein Kampf by Adolf Hitler
The Communist Manifesto by Karl Marx
The newest Harry Potter book
Science Magazine

Ask each of the following questions out loud and give students time to share their answers and interact with each other in their smaller groups.

- *Which item on the list have you read or watched the most?*
- *Which item have you never heard of?*
- *Which item on the list would you trust the least? Why?*
- *Which item on the list would you trust the most? Why?*
- *Which item would you trust the most for current news? Why?*
- *Which item on the list would you trust the most for life guidance? Why?*
- *Why would others trust something differently than you?*
- *Why should others make the same choice as you did?*

Point to the list again and transition by saying something like this—

There are people in the world who completely trust these information sources for guidance in life. Today we are going to look at why the Bible is our only reliable source for truth.

READ IT IN GOD'S WORD

"But as for you, continue in what you have learned and have become convinced of, because you know those from whom you learned it" (2 Timothy 3:14).

• By saying, "But as for you," Paul is comparing and contrasting the false teachers—whom he called "evil men" who were "deceiving" believers and "being deceived" by false teaching—in the previous verse.
• There's a difference between knowing intellectually and believing a doctrine or truth. Timothy believed what he was taught, and he believed in who taught him. In your faith and life, is there anything you have learned (have knowledge of) but you are not convinced of yet?

"And how from infancy you have known the Holy Scriptures, which are able to make you wise for salvation through faith in Christ Jesus" (2 Timothy 3:15).

ACTIVITY
WHERE IS IT?

You'll need—
- Copies of **Where Is It?** quiz (page 119) for each student
- Pen or pencil for each student
- Bibles
- Food prize (optional)

See how well your students know Scripture. Hand out the **Where Is It?** quiz (page 119) and something to write with. You can limit their time to make things more interesting or divide them up into teams to compete for a prize. Don't let them use their Bibles until the last minute of the time allowed. Give rewards to first team done and the team with the most correct answers.

The right answers are below:

1. B—Exodus 20
2. C—Genesis 3
3. A—Psalm 51
4. B—Judges 16
5. A—Matthew 6
6. A—Psalm 23
7. C—Luke 2
8. A—Matthew 5-7
9. D—Hebrews 11
10. D—John 17

• Jewish custom required a mother to begin training her children in the Scriptures at age five. After the children reached the age of 10 the father was responsible for their spiritual training. Timothy's father was Greek and probably not a believer. So Timothy's mother probably trained him in his faith for a longer period of time. What kind of spiritual foundation do you want to provide for your family one day?

• "Holy Scriptures" refers to the Old Testament. Scripture is not the way to salvation, but it points to it through Christ. It's a road sign that points toward the destination.

• Before you are a Christian, Scripture helps you know Christ initially. After you are a Christian, Scripture helps you know Christ intimately.

"All Scripture is God-breathed and is useful for teaching, rebuking, correcting and training in righteousness" (2 Timothy 3:16).

• "All Scripture" refers primarily to the Old Testament. However, at the time of this epistle, the Gospels had already been written and were being read in the churches, along with Paul's writings. In 2 Peter 3:15-16, Peter refers to Paul's writings as being Scripture on par with the Old Testament.

Does "all Scripture" really mean ALL Scripture? Is all Scripture useful in the same way? It helps to understand that different types or genres of Scripture exist and that they should be read differently.

Genre	Passage
History	Joshua 1
Narrative	Luke 2
Prophecy	Daniel 7
Poetry	Psalm 23
Proverbs	Proverbs 22:29
Parables	Luke 15:1-7
Epistle	James
Jesus' Sermon on the Mount	Matthew 5–7
Jesus' Parable of the Prodigal Son	Luke 15:11-32
Hyperbole	Matthew 23:24 ("You blind guides! You strain out a gnat but swallow a camel.")

All Scripture is inspired, but all Scripture isn't useful in every single situation. To understand the message of a text, first you have to know what kind of literature or genre it is. You read different genres of Scripture differently. And often there are many hurdles to jump—historical hurdles, language hurdles, cultural hurdles, time hurdles, and more—before we can discover the true message from various passages.

• When was it written?
• Who wrote it?
• Who was it written to?
• In what language was it written?
• What did it mean to the original readers?
• What does it mean to us in our world?
• What does it mean to me, right now?

• "God-breathed"—This is the best possible translation of the Greek word *theopneustos*.
• The image of something being God-breathed should remind us of God's role in the creation of Adam, as recorded in Genesis. According to Genesis 2:7, God breathed life into Adam's lifeless body. God's breath brought life into a physical body; God's breath into the Word (as alluded to in 2 Peter 1:21) gives life to what would otherwise be just a collection of letters.
• Scripture is useful for four things according to this verse, and although they are different things, they are all related. These four words incorporate two themes that Scripture is useful for—our doctrine and our life.

> Teaching (reinforcing sound doctrine)—Encouraging others to learn and be convinced of the truths of Scripture as God has revealed them to us. Know and believe sound doctrine.
> Rebuking (confronting faulty doctrine)—Encouraging others to avoid and stop believing things that don't measure up with the truths of Scripture as God has revealed them. Alter faulty doctrine.
> Correcting (confronting unhealthy living)—Encouraging others to stop living in ways that doesn't please God. Fix unhealthy living.
> Training in righteousness (reinforcing healthy living)—Encouraging others to start or continue living in a way that pleases God. Prepare for future health.

• "Above all, you must understand that no prophecy of Scripture came about by the prophet's own interpretation. For prophecy never had its origin in the will of man, but men spoke from God as they were carried along by the Holy Spirit" (2 Peter 1:20-21). The Greek word for *carried* is the image of the wind carrying a ship along by its sails.

You'll need—
• Copies of **My Bible Reading Plan** (page 120) for each student
• Pen or pencil for each student

Give students a copy of **My Bible Reading Plan** (page 120) and something to write with. Ask them to look over the 10 plans and choose one they can commit to following for the coming month. Plan to regularly email or call your students throughout the 30 days ahead to see how they're doing with their Bible reading.

"So that the man of God may be thoroughly equipped for every good work" (2 Timothy 3:17).

• We don't learn about God's truths (doctrine) just to know about them—we learn about them to put them into action! This was true for Timothy as a church leader and teacher; it was true for everyone in Ephesus; and it's true for us in our churches today.
• Until you do what you know is right, you don't know what you think you know. We must put our beliefs into action.
• How will you put this lesson and other lessons you hear into action?

"In the presence of God and of Christ Jesus, who will judge the living and the dead, and in view of his appearing and his kingdom, I give you this charge:" (2 Timothy 4:1)

• By saying "In the presence of God and of Christ Jesus," Paul is reminding the hearers that we are always in God's presence and that we should live our lives as if we were living them in front of the throne of God—because we are!
• "Who will judge the living and the dead"—Paul is reminding the hearers that God is the judge of all who are living and all who have ever lived, so we should live well for his sake.

"Preach the Word; be prepared in season and out of season; correct, rebuke and encourage—with great patience and careful instruction" (2 Timothy 4:2).

• This one verse contains a five-part command for Timothy:

  1. Preach the Word. This is the primary command upon which all the other commands are built.
  2. Be prepared in season and out of season. Preparation requires having a plan and acting upon a plan; Timothy didn't have a day off when he didn't have to be prepared.
  3. Correct. This involved helping someone correct something that they didn't know was wrong. Whether it was their beliefs or their behaviors, they were unaware of the problem.
  4. Rebuke. This involved helping someone correct something that they should have known was wrong, whether it was their beliefs or behaviors.
  5. Encourage. All believers need encouragement. Strong believers need it to continue in their faith and not to give up. Weaker believers need it so they won't give up in their faith but will grow stronger.

And all five of these commands were to be done with great patience and careful instruction.

"For the time will come when men will not put up with sound doctrine. Instead, to suit their own desires, they will gather around them a great number of teachers to say what their itching ears want to hear. They will

turn their ears away from the truth and turn aside to myths. But you, keep your head in all situations, endure hardship, do the work of an evangelist, discharge all the duties of your ministry" (2 Timothy 4:3-5).

• "For the time will come"—Even though Paul said it was *going to* happen, it already was happening. He had warned the church elders about this in Acts 20:29-30 when he said, "I know that after I leave, savage wolves will come in among you and will not spare the flock. Even from your own number men will arise and distort the truth in order to draw away disciples after them."

• These people searched for teachers who told them what they wanted to hear rather than what they needed to hear. "Itching ears" showed that they were curious for *new* tidbits of different thinking and that they were inclined to stray from what was normal. Instead of seeking truth they ran from truth.

• By saying, "But you" at the start of the sentence, Paul is once again telling Timothy not to be like the false teachers and false seekers. Instead he was to remain calm in all circumstances, share the Good News with others, carry out the other duties and responsibilities of his ministry, and not give up during hard times.

• During difficult times in our lives, we shouldn't use the hardships as an excuse to stop doing what is right and what is required of us.

ILLUSTRATION
TYNDALE'S TALE

Read the story on the **Tyndale's Tale** sheet (page 121) to your students. Ask for some reactions to the story. Were they surprised by how difficult it was to get a Bible translated into English? Or by how dedicated William Tyndale was to getting the translation made and printed?

LIVE IT IN YOUR WORLD

Share and discuss some of these different Bible-reading ideas with your students.

• Read the Bible quietly to contemplate
• Study the Bible in depth
• Read the Bible quickly for breadth
• Alone
• Together
• Read passages about particular topics
• Read books about the Bible
• Listen to it on tape
• Listen to sermons given about it
• Meditate—Choose one or two verses and think about them for five or 10 minutes
• Use the Internet and read eight different versions of a passage side by side
• Read the Bible in unison with friends

PUT IT IN YOUR HEART

"All Scripture is God-breathed and is useful for teaching, rebuking, correcting and training in righteousness" (2 Timothy 3:16).

SMALL GROUP QUESTIONS

1. How would your life change if you lived every moment as if you were standing, working, dating, and living in the throne room of God?

2. Could your patience be described as "great patience"? How could your patience become stronger?

3. If you became a prisoner of war and were not allowed to have a Bible, how many verses would you have *smuggled in* because you had them memorized?

4. Why do some people not trust the Bible?

5. Why do you trust the Bible?

6. Can you name a time when the Bible really seemed to be alive and active in your life?

7. Do you think it's a good thing or a goofy thing to have "Teen Bibles"? Explain.

8. You're not a preacher, so how can you preach the Word?

9. What was your first thought as you heard the statistics regarding the number of Bibles that are available in different languages around the world?

10. On a scale of 1-10, with 1 being "No way" and 10 being "I was going to do it anyway," please rank the following statements:
    • I'm open to helping other people own a copy of the Bible written in their own language.
    • One day I'd like to smuggle Bibles into countries that don't allow them.

CLOSING PRAYER

BIBLE NUMBERS

Use only the numbers provided below to fill in the blanks in the following paragraph about the Bible.

3 – 3 – 27 – 39 – 40 – 66 – 405 – 883 – 1,034 – 1,500 – 1,500 – 3,000

The Bible was written over _____ hundred years, by more than _____ men from very different walks of life. It was written under many different circumstances on _____ different continents and in _____ different languages. The writers had different purposes for writing, and they addressed a multitude of issues. Yet there is unity. That unity is organized around one theme: God's redemption of people and all of creation. The Bible, as we know it, is comprised of _____ different books, with _____ in the Old Testament and _____ in the New Testament. In 1999, Wycliffe Translators reported that of the 6,809 languages in the world, only _____ had an entire Bible translation in their own language; _____ had an adequate New Testament; _____ had some Scripture in their own language; there were _____ languages being translated at that time*; and over _____ different languages didn't have a copy of God's Word.

*This number represents Bible translation work as a whole, not just Wycliffe Bible Translators.

WHERE IS IT?

Circle the letter of the correct biblical location for each of the Bible stories or events.

1. God gives the 10 Commandments
A. Exodus 15
B. Exodus 20
C. Exodus 25
D. Exodus 30

2. Adam and Eve sinned
A. Genesis 1
B. Genesis 2
C. Genesis 3
D. Genesis 4

3. David's confessional prayer
A. Psalm 51
B. 1 Samuel 35
C. 2 Samuel 35
D. Psalm 15

4. Samson has a bad hair day (he gets a haircut)
A. Judges 17
B. Judges 16
C. Numbers 16
D. Numbers 17

5. Jesus teaches his disciples "The Lord's Prayer"
A. Matthew 6
B. Mark 6
C. Luke 6
D. John 6

6. The Lord is my shepherd
A. Psalm 23
B. Psalm 33
C. Psalm 43
D. Psalm 53

7. Jesus' birth
A. Matthew 1
B. Mark 1
C. Luke 2
D. John 2

8. The Sermon on the Mount
A. Matthew 5-7
B. Mark 5-7
C. Luke 5-7
D. John 5-7

9. The Christian hall of fame
A. Romans 11
B. 1 Corinthians 11
C. 2 Corinthians 11
D. Hebrews 11

10. Jesus prays with his disciples
A. Matthew 17
B. Mark 17
C. Luke 17
D. John 17

If you scored 0-3	**Don't worry—it's never to late to start reading your Bible!**
If you scored 3-6	**Either you're a good guesser, or you know your Bible.**
If you scored 7-9	**You definitely know your Bible.**
If you scored 10	**You know your Bible so well you should teach the next session!**

MY BIBLE READING PLAN

Which 30-day plan will I choose? (Read a chapter a day unless stated otherwise.)

1. A Proverb a day where the chapter number matches the day of the month

   _____

2. Two Psalms a day

   _____

3. Read the Gospel of Matthew

   _____

4. Read the book of Acts

   _____

5. Read 1 Corinthians and 2 Corinthians

   _____

6. Read two chapters of Genesis a day

   _____

7. Read 1 Samuel

   _____

8. Read Romans twice

   _____

9. Read Galatians through 2 Thessalonians

   _____

TYNDALE'S TALE

WILLIAM TYNDALE: THE NEW TESTAMENT A PLOUGHMAN COULD READ

How many Bibles do you have in your house? For most of us, Bibles are easily accessible, and many of us have several. That we have the Bible in English owes much to William Tyndale, sometimes called the Father of the English Bible. Ninety percent of the King James Version of the Bible and 75 percent of the Revised Standard Version are from the translation of the Bible into English made by William Tyndale, yet Tyndale himself was burned at the stake for his work on October 6, 1536.

Back in the 14th century, John Wycliffe was the first to make (or at least oversee) an English translation of the Bible, but that was before the invention of the printing press, and all copies had to be handwritten. Besides, the church had banned the unauthorized translation of the Bible into English in 1408.

Over one hundred years later, however, William Tyndale had a burning desire to make the Bible available to even the common people in England. After studying at Oxford and Cambridge, he joined the household of Sir John Walsh at Little Sudbury Manor as tutor to the Walsh children. Walsh was a generous lord of the manor and often entertained the local clergy at his table. Tyndale often added spice to the table conversation as he was confronted with the Biblical ignorance of the priests. At one point Tyndale told a priest, "If God spare my life, ere many years pass, I will cause a boy that driveth the plough shall know more of the Scriptures than thou dost."

It was a nice dream, but how was Tyndale to accomplish this when translating the Bible into English was illegal? He went to London to ask Bishop Tunstall if he could be authorized to make an English translation of the Bible, but the bishop would not grant his approval. But Tyndale would not let the disapproval of men stop him from carrying out what seemed so obviously God's will. With encouragement and support of some British merchants, he decided to go to Europe to complete his translation, then have it printed and smuggled back into England.

In 1524 Tyndale sailed for Germany. In Hamburg he worked on the New Testament, and in Cologne he found a printer who would print the work. However, news of Tyndale's activity came to an opponent of the Reformation who had the press raided. Tyndale himself managed to escape with the pages already printed and made his was to Worms where the New Testament was soon published. Six thousand copies were printed and smuggled into England. The bishops did everything they could to eradicate the Bibles—Bishop Tunstall had copies ceremoniously burned at St. Paul's; the archbishop of Canterbury bought up copies to destroy them. Tyndale used the money to print improved editions!

King Henry VIII, then in the throes of his divorce with Queen Katherine, offered Tyndale a safe passage to England to serve as his writer and scholar. Tyndale refused, saying he would not return until the Bible could be legally translated into English. Tyndale continued hiding among the merchants in Antwerp and began translating the Old Testament into English while the King's agents searched all over England and Europe for him.

Tyndale was finally found by an Englishman who pretended to be his friend but then turned him over to the authorities. After a year and a half in prison, he was brought to trial for heresy—for believing, among other things, in the forgiveness of sins and that the mercy offered in the gospel was enough for salvation. In August 1536 he was condemned, and on October 6, 1536, he was strangled and his body burned at the stake. His last prayer was, "Lord, open the King of England's eyes." The prayer was answered in part when three years later, in 1539, Henry VIII required every parish church in England to make a copy of the English Bible available to its parishioners. (© Christian History Institute, www.chinstitute.org, used with permission.)

From Creative Bible Lessons in 1 & 2 Timothy and Titus by Len Evans. Permission to reproduce this page granted only for use in buyer's own youth group. ©2004 by Youth Specialties. www.YouthSpecialties.com

good works

PUTTING YOUR FAITH INTO ACTION

session 12

During this session students will—

- Discuss and discern how to put their faith into action by doing good works.
- Evaluate the good works of their church and youth ministry.
- Make plans to improve what they're already doing or implement some new ways to serve others.

THE BIG IDEA

Believers need to be reminded to do good works.

BACKGROUND CHECK

Overall, the book of Titus is similar to 1 Timothy, but this section (along with Titus 2:6-15) is very distinct. Again we don't know much about Titus, but we know he served as pastor of the church in Crete, the southernmost Greek island in the eastern Mediterranean Sea. Paul left Titus there to continue the ministry Paul had started and to appoint elders.

A historian writes, "Cretans were notorious for a revolutionary spirit." These rebellious people were the faithful ones in the church, and they had been changed by the grace of God, which is also explained well in this passage. Christians of the first century were not easily accepted because others viewed them as a sect of Judaism that didn't follow the cultural norms. For these reasons and more, people were often suspicious of Christians. Paul encourages the Christians in Crete to live out their faith through good works in their society. The term *good works* is used three times in the first 15 verses of the third chapter of Titus. Paul was trying to make a point by repeating this theme so many times within such a small passage—a good reputation follows good works.

OPENING
Option 1: The Nobody Wins Contest

You'll need—
• An index card for each student
• Pen or pencil for each student
• A prize for everyone

Give each student an index card and a pen. Read them the following instructions—

Number your card one through six. You'll write your answers on the card as I read each of the questions. I will ask each question only once. After the last question is read, you will have 10 seconds to bring me your cards but only if you have answered all six questions. The winner will get a prize.

(Note: No one is going to win, but it's important that you give a prize of some sort to every person—a bag of candy to share or $5 off your next event fee.) The six questions are below:

1. What's the square root of 1,764? (42)
2. What day did Texas join the United States of America? (December 29, 1845)
3. What third baseman has the most career home runs? (Mike Schmidt)
4. What's the shortest verse in the Bible? (John 11:35)
5. What is the first stock listed on the New York Stock Exchange? (Agilent Technologies Inc.)
6. What was the 36th most popular name for girls born in America in 1999? (Stephanie)

Read each question again and ask students to shout out their answers. Then read the right answer. Now transition into the lesson by saying something like—

This was a contest that no one could win, but I'm going to give everyone a prize. It's not because you earned it but because I want to show you undeserved kindness. Undeserved kindness is something that God offers to us, and in the Bible it's called grace. Let's look at what Paul shared with Titus regarding the importance of grace and our response to it.

Option 2: The Sacred or Secular Quiz
It's a common perspective among people that some things are considered sacred and other things are considered secular. Sacred is simply defined as "of God" or "holy", while secular is something "of the world" or "earthly." Say each of the following job titles out loud—missionary, plumber, homemaker, pastor, actress, athlete, teacher, Bible professor, stripper, musician—and then ask, "Is this job sacred or secular?" Ask the students to respond with a show of hands for each choice.

Transition into the lesson by saying something like—

Some people believe that the world, events, and actions can easily be categorized as being sacred or secular. Others believe that if you are a believer, most of life is sacred. How you fold your clothes should be sacred, how you talk to your teachers and parents should be sacred, and whatever you eventually do for a living should be sacred. Paul gave Titus instructions to remind the believers that they should be putting their faith into action and doing good works for their neighbors and community.

READ IT IN GOD'S WORD

"Remind the people to be subject to rulers and authorities, to be obedient, to be ready to do whatever is good" (Titus 3:1).

• Even the churches where the apostle Paul served as a pastor had to be reminded of all the things he had said and the basic truths of the gospel. They also had to be reminded to do what they knew. If you know what you need to do but you don't do it, do you really know it?

• "The people" were the believers in the local church, not the citizens of Crete. Christians, not non-Christians, are held to the standard of Christian behavior.

• Christians in Ephesus were reminded to pray for their rulers (1 Timothy 2:1-3); those in Crete were reminded to obey their rulers. By obeying the rulers that God has established, we also obey God (Romans 13:1-7 and 1 Peter 2:13-15). Our attitudes toward authorities reveal our attitude toward God.

• "To be ready to do whatever is good"—Elsewhere we are told to do good to everyone, especially to those who belong in the family of believers (Galatians 6:9-10). But here the emphasis is to do good things to those outside the church.

• Christians should be responsible citizens. Bob Briner, author of *Roaring Lambs*, encouraged believers to be active in culture and society. He believed and taught that our greatest ministry opportunity to those who don't believe is by simply being involved with the world and doing our best at whatever we do.

• Believers should show mercy and compassion by being among the many people who donate blood, work in soup kitchens, raise money for cancer research, and more. We've been promised a home in an eternal world, so we should love and serve those here in our earthly home.

ACTIVITY
TO OBEY OR DISOBEY? THAT IS THE QUESTION!

You'll need—
• Copies of **To Obey or Disobey? That Is the Question!** (page 128) for each student
• Pen or pencil for each student

Hand out **To Obey or Disobey? That Is the Question!** (page 128) and something to write with to each student. Give them five minutes to read the statements and circle their responses. Then go over each statement and ask students to share their thoughts about each.

And if you've ever participated in an act of civil disobedience, you may wish to share a story or two with your students. Just be sure the main point of this section (regarding how our attitudes toward authority figures reflect our attitude toward God) isn't lost in the telling.

"To slander no one, to be peaceable and considerate, and to show true humility toward all men" (Titus 3:2).

• Watch your words. Don't talk badly about others. Slander and gossip are similar in that they both involve spoken words—which can be negative—that may or may not be true about another person.

• "Peaceable"—As the old saying goes, "You don't have to attend every argument that you're invited to."

• **"If it is possible, as far as it depends on you, live at peace with everyone"** (Romans 12:18).

• *Considerate* comes from the same Greek word as *meek*, which can be used to describe a powerful horse that has been broken—it was once wild, but now it can be ridden. The power is now under control.

• Paul again emphasizes that these commands are to be practiced toward all people—believers and unbelievers. It reflects the same principle that Jesus commanded when he said, **"Love your neighbor as yourself"** (Luke 10:27).

"At one time we too were foolish, disobedient, deceived and enslaved by all kinds of passions and pleasures. We lived in malice and envy, being hated and hating one another" (Titus 3:3).

• When Paul writes "we too," he reminds them of what their lives were like before they had faith. Pride is always a danger for everyone, including believers, but if you remember your life before Jesus, you won't be prideful of where you are now. Paul never forgot what God did for him through Christ: "Here is a trustworthy saying that deserves full acceptance: Christ Jesus came into the world to save sinners—of whom I am the worst. But for that very reason I was shown mercy so that in me, the worst of sinners, Christ Jesus might display his unlimited patience as an example for those who would believe on him and receive eternal life" (1 Timothy 1:15-16).

• We should show compassion to our unbelieving friends, not contempt or condemnation. There is an old saying that you may not have heard before: "As believers when we share our faith with someone else, we are just like a beggar telling another beggar where to find the bread."

• When a hungry person finds food, she wants to share with other hungry friends and tell them where they can find food, too. That's all we are doing when we go to our friends and talk to them in normal and natural ways about the good we've found in Christ.

"But when the kindness and love of God our Savior appeared" (Titus 3:4).

• In the Greek, verses four through seven are one complete sentence! Because it says so much in such a small amount of space, it was possibly an early doctrinal creed either written by Paul or recognized by Paul to share with believers.

ACTIVITY
CREATE YOUR OWN CREED

You'll need—
• Copies of **Create Your Own Creed** (page 129) for each student
• Pen or pencil for each student

Pass out **Create Your Own Creed** (page 129) to your students, along with something to write with. Then say—

Christians have condensed their beliefs into short statements, often called creeds, since the early days of the church. We have examples of them throughout church history, but more importantly, Paul gave us a few condensed statements of faith in his New Testament epistles.

Now ask a few students to read aloud these statements found in Philippians 2:6-11, Titus 3:4-7, and 1 Timothy 1:15-17. Then continue by saying—

The most common creed is the Apostles' Creed. Creeds are not magical, nor are they equal to Scripture, but they do remind us of the important things we believe from Scripture. Let's read the Apostles' Creed out loud together.

After you've finished suggest that your students take 10 or 15 minutes to read through the next creed on the page (Youth Specialties' "We believe in Jesus" statement) on their own. This one will give them an idea of what a more modern-sounding creed might look like. Once they've read it they should begin to work—individually—on crafting their own creeds. Give them some ideas about the types of beliefs they may wish to include in their creeds.

When time is up, ask a few students to share their modern-day creeds with the rest of the group. You may wish to post a few of them somewhere in your youth group room or even on your group's Web site for a week or two.

• The Greek word for love in this verse is *philanthropia*. It is best translated "Love toward man." Because God was full of kindness and felt love toward people, the Savior appeared.

• "Savior appeared" refers to Emmanuel or God with us, Jesus Christ who came down to earth to care for and express his love for people of all time.

"He saved us, not because of righteous things we had done, but because of his mercy. He saved us through the washing of rebirth and renewal by the Holy Spirit" (Titus 3:5).

• "Saved us" is the primary subject of the entire sentence, as well as the primary subject of our faith. It is written in the past tense because it is an historical event. Our salvation is in the past because of what Jesus has done for us.

• No one can do enough good things to make God love them and accept them. Even in the Old Testament it was understood that our good works were filthy rags (Isaiah 64:6). And the English term *filthy rags* is not even descriptive enough. In the original language, the Hebrew word that was used here was the same word used for the rags that had been used to clean off diseases or bloody wounds. That's what our good works are worth (Ephesians 2:8-9).

• "Renewal" implies a continuing activity rather than an activity from the past. So we were saved because of what Christ did on the cross and his resurrection, but we are also being saved (becoming more and more like Christ) in our present life. Philippians 2:12 says, "Continue to work out your salvation with fear and trembling."

• Salvation began for the world when Jesus came down in his mercy, died on the cross, and rose again.

• Salvation begins for each person when they believe in Jesus' message, his work upon the cross, and his resurrection.

"Whom he poured out on us generously through Jesus Christ our Savior, so that, having been justified by his grace, we might become heirs having the hope of eternal life" (Titus 3:6-7).

• Grace is always the centerpiece at our table of faith—you can't miss it. People can invent ways for us to work to get to Heaven, but only God could initiate grace as an invitation to Heaven. Lewis Sperry Chafer expressed this idea even better when he wrote, "Anyone can devise a plan by which good people go to heaven. Only God can devise a plan whereby sinners, which are His enemies, can go to heaven."

• Heirs can't inherit anything until someone dies. Instead of waiting for someone to die so I can live a better life upon receiving a financial inheritance, my greatest inheritance occurs when I die and my hope of eternal life is realized firsthand!

DID YOU NOTICE?

The word *trinity* is not found in the Bible; however, the truth of God being one God and yet three persons is clearly seen in the New Testament and hinted at in the Old Testament. Verses 5 and 6 show that God the Father, God the Son, and God the Spirit all work simultaneously and yet distinctly to offer and give us salvation. (See also Matthew 28:19-20.)

"This is a trustworthy saying. And I want you to stress these things, so that those who have trusted in God may be careful to devote themselves to doing what is good. These things are excellent and profitable for everyone... Our people must learn to devote themselves to doing what is good, in order that they may provide for daily necessities and not live unproductive lives" (Titus 3:8, 14).

• "Devote themselves" implies that good works will be initiated by believers. These were to be intentional acts of goodness. Good works profit those who do them and those who receive them. How good are we with our good works?

LIVE IT IN YOUR WORLD

ACTIVITY
DOING GOOD WORKS

You'll need—
- Copies of **Doing Good Works** (page 130) for each group
- Pen or pencil for each group

Divide the students into groups of four to five and give each group a copy of **Doing Good Works** (page 130) and something to write with. Ask them to work together on answering the questions and brainstorming some ideas for service projects that their small group or the youth group as a whole could do in the next month or so.

After about 15 minutes ask some of the groups to share their ideas with everyone. Plan to implement some of them or encourage the small groups to follow through on one of their ideas (with an adult leader, if possible). Then at a future meeting you could plan to have all the groups who did a service project report back to the group about what they did and how the people they served responded. Encourage them to take pictures or videotape their service project so they can share these experiences with the rest of the students sometime.

PUT IT IN YOUR HEART

"This is a trustworthy saying. And I want you to stress these things, so that those who have trusted in God may be careful to devote themselves to doing what is good. These things are excellent and profitable for everyone" (Titus 3:8).

SMALL GROUP QUESTIONS

1. Is it ever right to disobey the rules that God has established?
2. Do you agree with the *Roaring Lambs* mind-set, or should believers pursue primarily sacred careers?
3. As students what could you do to be more involved with your school and local community events?
4. Are you more Christian or more American?
5. What influences you more—your Christianity or your culture?
6. Has someone ever slandered you or your reputation? What did it feel like? Was it ever resolved?
7. What could your youth ministry do to serve your church's neighbors (the community around your church)?
8. It's often said of Christians that they are too arrogant. How can you be confident of your faith and yet share it humbly with others?
9. Do you view yourself as being the worst of sinners? Why did Paul say that he was the worst of sinners?

CLOSING PRAYER

TO OBEY OR DISOBEY? THAT IS THE QUESTION!

Circle one response for each statement below.

1. Christians should obey the speed limit.
   yes   no   maybe   doesn't apply

2. Christians should pay their income taxes.
   yes   no   maybe   doesn't apply

3. Martin Luther King, Jr. was right to break the laws he broke because he did it to bring about the same civil rights for all Americans.
   yes   no   maybe   doesn't apply

4. Nathaniel Heatwole, a college student who smuggled box cutters onto two Southwest Airlines jetliners in 2003, was right to break the laws he broke because he wanted to improve public safety for the air-traveling public.
   yes   no   maybe   doesn't apply

5. Christians in China should break the laws that forbid them to meet as a church and read the Bible.
   yes   no   maybe   doesn't apply

6. Christians should follow the school dress code even if they don't like it.
   yes   no   maybe   doesn't apply

7. If other T-shirts are allowed, Christians should wear Christian T-shirts with messages—even if the school has banned it.
   yes   no   maybe   doesn't apply

8. If all T-shirts are banned by the school dress code, a Christian should wear a Christian T-shirt and declare "freedom of speech" as an act of civil disobedience.
   yes   no   maybe   doesn't apply

9. It's okay for a believer to cheat on a test if it's just for one answer.
   yes   no   maybe   doesn't apply

10. It's okay to be late for curfew as long as you went to a Bible study.
    yes   no   maybe   doesn't apply

11. If your 21st birthday is in two weeks, it's okay to drink alcohol.
    yes   no   maybe   doesn't apply

Our attitudes toward authorities reveal our attitude toward God.

CREATE YOUR OWN CREED

Read "The Apostles' Creed" and "We Believe in Jesus." Then take 10-15 minutes to think and write down the important things that you believe.

The Apostles' Creed (Modern English Version)

I believe in God, the Father almighty,
Creator of heaven and earth.

I believe in Jesus Christ, God's only Son, our Lord,
Who was conceived by the Holy Spirit and
born of the Virgin Mary.
He suffered under Pontius Pilate,
was crucified, died, and was buried.
He descended to the dead.
On the third day he rose again.
He ascended into heaven,
and is seated at the right hand of the Father.
He will come again to judge the living and the dead.

I believe in the Holy Spirit,
the holy catholic Church*,
the communion of saints,
the forgiveness of sins,
the resurrection of the body,
and the life everlasting. Amen.

*catholic Church = universal Church

We believe in Jesus.

We know He's part of the Trinity and all the other important stuff we also believe, but if we're honest, we're partial to Jesus. Don't get us wrong. God is like a Father—no, God IS the Father—and the buck stops with him (if you're going to have the buck stop somewhere it might as well stop with someone who is, well, all about love with a capital L. Of course, he's also about justice with a capital J, but we'll take our chances that, in the end, justice will feel like love). And then there is the Holy Spirit—mysterious, windy, seems to like fire a lot, whispering, and always pointing us to, you guessed it, Jesus. We not only like Jesus a lot, He likes us a lot. Enough to die for us. We know that when life gets tough (and it always does), He'll be there for us (from "Important Stuff Youth Specialties Believes" at www.youthspecialties.com).

What Do YOU Believe?
(Write it here!)

_____

_____

_____

_____

_____

_____

DOING GOOD WORKS
WHAT HAVE WE DONE?

Good Works of our Church   **Good Works of our Youth Ministry**

1.   1.

2.   2.

3.   3.

4.   4.

5.   5.

1. Are these mostly planned or spontaneous?

2. What grade would you give your church for good works?

3. What grade would you give your youth ministry for good works?

4. What more do we need to do?

5. How often should we do these things?

6. How can we get others involved?

Ideas to Consider

Visit www.kindness.com and discover more about servant evangelism.

Visit www.souperbowl.org and see how your church can annually support a local soup kitchen.

Visit www.30hourfamine.org and see how you can help partner with World Vision to feed hungry children.

Visit www.compassion.com or www.worldvision.org and look into supporting a child for a year.

BIBLIOGRAPHY

Barton, Bruce B., David R. Veerman, and Neil Wilson. *Life Application Bible Commentary: 1 Timothy, 2 Timothy and Titus*. Wheaton, IL: Tyndale House Publishers Inc., 1993.

DeMarest, Gary W. *Mastering the New Testament: 1, 2 Thessalonians; 1, 2 Timothy; and Titus*. Waco, TX: Word Inc, 1984.

Earle, Ralph. *Word Meanings in the New Testament*. Peabody, MA: Hendrickson Publishers, 1997.

Earle, Ralph. *The Expositor's Bible Commentary, Vol 11*. Grand Rapids, MI: Zondervan, 1978.

Fee, Gordon D. *New International Biblical Commentary: 1 and 2 Timothy, Titus*. Peabody, MA: Hendrickson Publishers, 1993.

Griffiths, Michael. *Timothy and Titus*. Grand Rapids, MI: Baker Books, 1996.

Jordan, Clarence. *The Cotton Patch Version of Paul's Epistles*. New York, NY: Association Press, 1970.

Keener, Craig S. *The IVP Bible Background Commentary: New Testament*. Downers Grove, IL: Inter-Varsity Press, 1994.

Knight, George W., III. *New International Greek Testament Commentary: The Pastoral Epistles*. Grand Rapids, MI: Eerdmans, 1992.

Liefeld, Walter L. *The NIV Application Commentary: 1 & 2 Timothy/Titus*. Grand Rapids, MI: Zondervan, 1999.

MacArthur, John. *The MacArthur New Testament Commentary: 1 Timothy*. Chicago, IL: Moody, 1995.

MacArthur, John. *The MacArthur New Testament Commentary: 2 Timothy*. Chicago, IL: Moody, 1995.

MacArthur, John. *The MacArthur New Testament Commentary: Titus*. Chicago, IL: Moody, 1996.

Milne, Douglas J. W. *1 and 2 Timothy and Titus (Focus on the Bible Commentary Series)*. Great Britain: Christian Focus Publications Ltd., 1996.

Stott, John R. W., *Guard the Gospel: The Message of 2 Timothy*. Downers Grove, IL: Inter-Varsity Press, 1973.

Walvoord, John F., and Roy B. Zuck. *The Bible Knowledge Commentary: An Exposition of the Scriptures by Dallas Seminary Faculty – New Testament*. Wheaton, IL: Scripture Press Publications, Victor Books, 1983.

Wiersbe, Warren W. *The Bible Exposition Commentary: Volume 2*. Wheaton, IL: Scripture Press Publications, Victor Books, 1983.

Yaconelli, Mike, ed. *Stories of Emergence: Moving from Absolute to Authenticity*. Grand Rapids, MI: Zondervan, 2003.